Mother Goose Goes to School

Goes to School

More than 100 Rhymes and Activities

BOB BARTON

❀

DAVID BOOTH

Pembroke Publishers Limited

We are indebted to the work of Iona and Peter Opie, who have rescued the lore and language of childhood from disappearing into the invisible past; and to the staff of the Osborne Collection in Toronto.

© 1995 Pembroke Publishers
538 Hood Road
Markham, Ontario, Canada L3R 3K9

Canadian Cataloguing in Publication Data

Barton, Robert, 1939-
  Mother Goose goes to school

Includes bibliographical references and index.
ISBN 1-55138-056-0

1. Nursery rhymes. 2. Elementary school teaching.
I. Booth, David. II. Title.

LB1044.88.B37 1995   372.13'2   C95-932247-7

A catalogue record for this book is available from the British Library.
Published in the U.K. by
Drake Educational Associates
St. Fagan's Road, Fairwater, Cardiff CF5 3AE

Editor: David Kilgour
Design: John Zehethofer
Cover Illustration: Pat Cupples
Typesetting: Jay Tee Graphics Ltd.

Printed and bound in Canada by Webcom
9 8 7 6 5 4 3 2

CONTENTS

PREFACE

Mother Goose Is a Teacher

For many, many years, Mother Goose has played a large role in our work in schools. Since a lot of the traditional nursery rhymes were unfamiliar to some children, we wanted the opportunity for them to feel the rhythms and try on the words as pleasurably as possible. And we have found that even though archaic words and expressions and odd vocabulary fill the rhymes, they seldom pose any barriers to the children's delight and understanding. The images created by the nursery rhymes are powerful and evocative, and the characters we meet in them stay with us throughout our lives. The stories the rhymes tell (or hint at) are rich with possibilities for the children's own storymaking, at any age, in any grade.

In this book, there are a hundred rhymes, many new to the children (and perhaps to you), drawn from centuries of literary remnants collected by both chance and design. For those of you working with children in school, we hope this will be a valuable resource for language teaching, full of rhyming patterns, unusual words, juxtaposed ideas, implied stories, archetypal characters. We delight in discovering with children the unknown verses, the chants and calls and lullabies that need voices to bring them to life. And of course the children can write their own poems, tell their own stories, paint their own pictures — stimulated by the lore of Mother Goose, right inside the classroom. Mother Goose can amuse and entertain and instruct in different ways throughout childhood, and she will lodge deep in the memory.

Dan Jones

ALL ABOUT MOTHER GOOSE

Who Was Mother Goose?

Cackle cackle, Mother goose
Have you any feathers loose?
Truly have I pretty fellow
Half enough to fill a pillow
Here are quills, take one or two,
And down to make a bed for you.

For years, we have been intrigued with the rhymes of Mother Goose, and with the historical facts, stories, and legends which attempt to explain their origins. Folklorist Andrew Lang said they were "smooth stones from the brook of time, worn round by constant friction of tongues long silent." In truth, we don't know the origins of most of these rhymes. While writers have attempted to find the original meanings of all the old verses, their work is often misdirected and sometimes just guesswork. We can trace some words and phrases, the names of people and places and historical events, but much lies buried in time. The name "Mother Goose" dates from 1697, when Charles Perrault published a collection of fairy tales, not poems, called *Les Contes de ma mère l'oye* (*Tales of My Mother Goose*). "Mother Goose" appeared in England as a book of fairy tales published in 1729, and the term 'nursery rhyme' appeared in the nineteenth century. In America, nursery rhymes were known as 'Mother Goose songs'. But we have to remember that, whether we call them Mother Goose rhymes or something else, these verses have endured hundreds of years. For example, the riddle "White Bird Featherless" appears in Latin in the tenth century. The English version is:

White bird featherless,
Flew from paradise,
Pitched on the garden wall.
Along came Lord Landless,
Took it up handless,
And rode away horseless,
to the King's white hall.
(Answer: a snowflake)

A French version of "Thirty Days Hath September" belongs to the thirteenth century. Some of the rhymes were well known when Shakespeare was a child, and are referred to in his plays. "Pat-a-Cake, Baker's Man" was included in D'Urfey's comedy *The Campaigners*, two-and-a-half centuries ago, when the nurse sang:

Ah Doddy blesse dat pitty face of myn Sylds, and his pitty, pitty hands, and his pitty, pitty foots, and all his pitty things, and pat a cake, pat a cake Bakers man, so I will master as I can, and prick it, and prick it, and prick it, and prick it, and prick, and throw't into the oven.

Where are the beginnings of this next gem?

Baa Baa black sheep
Have you any wool?
Yes, sir, Yes, sir,
Three bags full.
One for the master
And one for the dame
And one for the little boy
Who lives down the lane.

Jean Harrowven in *Origins of Rhymes, Songs and Sayings* provides us with speculation about this common rhyme.

England wouldn't permit the export of wool from the country as raw wool, but insisted on selling it as piece goods. The weavers in the cottages tried to save as much of the wool for themselves as possible by stretching the material and providing a certain length without using all of the raw wool. The one bag for the master is actually that woven into material, and the one bag for the dame was the amount they saved by fraudulent means. In 1275 an export tax was imposed on wool, so the one bag for the little boy who lives down the lane was the amount needed to pay the tax collector. At that time black sheep were much sought after, as it was possible to make black stockings without dying the yarn. So the masters were accused of trying to keep all the black wool for themselves.

But what of the rhyme's beginnings? Did it satirize the event, or did the words and patterns evolve from the leftover gossip of a long-forgotten episode? Does it matter? Bits and pieces of these verses were originally authored by poets, playwrights, politicians, and actors, in music halls, in plays, in political satire. Over the years, lines were altered and verses added. Except for the lullabies, most rhymes were never originally intended for children. For example:

> Rub-a-dub-dub,
> Three men in a tub
> And who do you think they be?
> The butcher, the baker,
> The candlestick-maker,
> Turn them out, knaves all three.

This apparently referred to three country maids half-submerged in a tub, a primitive form of striptease in country fairs, ogled at through a peep-hole by the butcher, the baker, and the candlestick-maker. The original story was altered so that it was these three characters who appeared in the tub instead of the maids. However, children don't need historical explanations in order to enjoy such rhymes.

Dennis Lee leaves the origin of this rhyme far behind as he sails to sea in a bathtub.

> I'm sailing to sea in the bathroom,
>   And I'm swimming to sea in a tub,
> And the only song that I ever will sing
>   is rub-a-dub dub-a-dub dub.
>
> A duck and a dog and a submarine
>   Are sailing together with me,
> And it's rub-a-dub-dub
> And it's dub-a-dub-dub
>   As we all sail out to sea.

This small children's fortune-telling rhyme was used when counting cherry stones, waistcoat buttons, daisy petals, or seeds, and sometimes when skipping;

Tinker,
  Tailor,
Soldier,
  Sailor
Rich man,
  Poor man,
Beggarman,
  Thief.

There are many variations in the ending, such as "Gentleman, apothecary, ploughboy, thief," and the rhyme is echoed in this nursery poem:

Lady, lady on the seashore,
She has children one to four,
The eldest one is twenty-four,
Then she shall marry a tinker, tailor, etc.

Was Little Boy Blue intended to represent Cardinal Wolsey, the son of an Ipswich butcher who looked after his father's livestock?

Little Boy Blue,
  Come blow your horn,
The sheep's in the meadow,
  The cow's in the corn;
But where is the boy
  Who looks after the sheep?
He's under a haycock,
  Fast asleep.

Will you wake him?
  No, not I,
For if I do,
  He's sure to cry.

Nursery rhyme anthologists Peter and Iona Opie tell us that a careful search of the original edition of *The Tragedy of Cardinal Wolsey* has failed to produce anything more resembling the rhyme than,

O fie on wolves, that march in masking-clothes,
For to devour the lambs, when shepherd sleeps.

A more likely allusion occurs in *King Lear* when Edgar, talking in his character of mad Tom, cries:

Sleepest or wakest thou, jolly shepherd?
   Thy sheepe bee in the corne;
And for one blast of thy minikin mouth
   Thy sheepe shall take no harme.

The Opies have recorded theories about the popular rhyme "Sing a Song of Sixpence", including: i) the twenty-four blackbirds are the hours of the day; the king the sun; the queen the moon; ii) the blackbirds are the choirs of about-to-be-dissolved monasteries making a dainty pie for Henry VIII; the queen is Katharine of Aragon, the maid Anne Boleyn; iii) the king, again, is Henry VIII; the rye, tribute in kind; the birds, twenty-four manorial title-deeds presented under a crust; iv) the maid is a sinner; the blackbird, the demon snapping off the maid's nose to reach her soul; v) the printing of the English Bible is celebrated, blackbirds being the letters of the alphabet which were 'baked in a pie' when set up by the printers in pica form. In an Italian cookery book from 1549, there is a recipe "to make pies so that the birds may be alive in them and flie out when it is cut up". This dish is further referred to (1723) by John Nott, cook to the Duke of Bolton, as a practice of former days, the purpose of the birds being to put out the candles and so cause a "diverting Hurley-Burley amongst the Guests in the Dark". It is well known that in the sixteenth century surprising things were inserted in pies, as in the legend which attaches itself to the rhyme "Jack Horner". The mention of a "counting-house", much referred to in *The Merry Wives of Windsor*, also helps to indicate that the rhyme may be traced to the sixteenth century, and the "pocket full of rye" may be the specific "pocket" sack-measurement of that grain. A further verse is from 1866: "They sent for the King's doctor, who sewed it on again, He sewed it on so neatly, the seam was never seen; and the jackdaw for his naughtiness deservedly was slain." In 1880, Randolph Caldecott added the couplet, "but there came a Jenny Wren and popped it on again."

Sing a song of sixpence,
    A pocket full of rye;
Four and twenty blackbirds,
    Baked in a pie.

When the pie was opened,
    The birds began to sing;
Was not that a dainty dish,
    To set before the king?

The king was in his counting-house,
    Counting out his money;
The queen was in the parlour,
    Eating bread and honey.

The maid was in the garden,
    Hanging out the clothes,
There came a little blackbird,
    And snapped off her nose.

One of the best known poems in the English language was
written by Jane Taylor and appeared in *Rhymes for the Nursery*
in 1806. You may not be aware of all the verses.

Twinkle, twinkle, little star,
How I wonder what you are!
Up above the world so high,
Like a diamond in the sky.

When the blazing sun is gone,
When he nothing shines upon,
Then you show your little light,
Twinkle, twinkle, all the night.

Then the traveller in the dark,
Thanks you for your tiny spark,
He could not see which way to go,
If you did not twinkle so.

In the dark blue sky you keep,
And often through my curtains peep,
For you never shut your eye,
Till the sun is in the sky.

As your bright and tiny spark,
Lights the traveller in the dark —
Though I know not what you are,
Twinkle, twinkle, little star.

It has been frequently parodied, as in Lewis Carroll's Mad Hatter's song:

Twinkle, twinkle, little bat!
How I wonder what you're at!
Up above the world you fly,
Like a tea-tray in the sky.

The inhabitant of a nursery rhyme shoe has been identified with several women because of the size of their families.

There was an old woman who lived in a shoe,
She had so many children she didn't know what to do;
She gave them some broth without any bread;
She whipped them all soundly and put them to bed.

The Opies tell us the shoe was symbolic of "what is personal to a woman until marriage. Casting a shoe after the bride when she goes off on her honeymoon is possibly a relic of this, symbolizing the wish that the union shall be fruitful. This is consistent with the many children belonging to a woman who actually lived in a shoe."

A Scottish version goes, "There was a wee bit wifie, Who lived in a shoe; She had so many bairns, She kenn'd what to do. She gaed to the market To buy a sheep-head; When she came back They were a 'lying dead. She went to the wright To get them a coffin; When she came back They were a' lyin laughing. She gaed up the stair, To ring the bell; The bell-rope broke, And down she fell." But Beatrix Potter in 1918 wrote, "You know the old woman who lived in a shoe? And had so many children She didn't know what to do? I think if she lived in a little shoe-house — That little old woman was surely a mouse!"

The songs, riddles, stories, lullabies, charms, counting-out rhymes, dances, nonsense verse, and proverbs which comprise the material known as Mother Goose have been part of a strong tradition of telling aloud, and this body of work is so hardy, so memorable, that it has continued to be reworked and developed into our own time. Undoubtedly the combination of toe-tapping rhythm and rhyme along with fantastical story plots has been largely responsible for the popularity of the nursery rhymes, but so too has their subject matter. One of this century's most successful illustrators of nursery rhymes, Raymond Briggs, was drawn to them because they were "quite rude, quite tough, adult, gutsy material about money and marriage and work and laziness and theft — not sweet innocent pink and blue baby stuff." True, the rhymes depict the rough edges of human existence, but they also possess extraordinary richness, beauty, and mystery. They can have a profound influence on children from a very early age. "The best of the older ones," says Robert Graves, "are nearer to poetry than the greater part of *The Oxford Book of English Verse.*"

Rhymes in the Playground

Vegetable Love,
Do you carrot all for me?
My heart beets for you.
With your turnip nose
And your radish face,
You are a peach.
If we cantaloupe,
Lettuce marry;
Weed make a swell pear.

At play, we can hear children calling out skipping rhymes, jingles, riddles, sayings, superstitions, taunts and teases, cat-calls and retorts, autograph verses, street songs, counting-out rhymes, ball-bounce chants, tongue twisters, join-in rhythms, action songs, nonsense verses, lullabies, jokes, silly rhymes, parodies, nicknames, slogans, ads, all shouted and sung in the freedom of the playground. These verses form the folk poetry of childhood. We may recognize a phrase from a television show, a tune from an advertisement, a line from a cartoon, a rhyme from a song; there may be a rude expression for an enemy, a city with an interesting-sounding name, an alphabet rhyme for choosing who is first, a counting verse for deciding who was last, a friend's name made into a rhyme. Like magic, these creations alter overnight, springing up anew on an unsuspecting playground in some other city. As Margaret Meek writes:

All these old chants and verses that we seem to dredge up from early memories to pass on to our children are the rags and bones of a once flourishing oral tradition of folklore and song, one that our newer print-soaked society has driven underground or transformed into television jingles and other kinds of popular culture.

When people immigrated to North America from all over the English-speaking world, they brought with them very few possessions but all kinds of memories, and the children added their voices to the streets and schoolyards of their new homes. Some of these words are still shouted and sung today, while other rhymes have faded into the past. When we see the verses written down, we can hear bits and pieces from centuries of nursery rhymes. We recently watched a group of twelve-year-old girls reading the poems and laughing at their past lives, arguing about the various versions they had experienced, adding verses, and sharing other songs and verses recently relegated to childhood past.

For teachers, these "other nursery rhymes" written on the streets and playgrounds of urban centres, free from adult interference, can provide an important bridge between the children and the poetry of books and school.

Hitchhiking on Nursery Rhymes

Contemporary poets have often taken the well known rhymes, the slapstick humour, the wit, and the comic spirit of Mother Goose and borrowed them for their own writing. At the turn of the century, much of the poetry written for children was sentimental, even patronizing, but today's poets write verse that is often light-hearted and vigorous, echoing childhood's chants and cheers. The best of it, such as that of Dennis Lee, Jack Prelutsky, Sheree Fitch, and Shel Silverstein, is simple and well crafted, incorporating the oral traditions of playground verse and the cadences of Mother Goose. These poets use sound patterns that have the satisfying rhyme of the memory gems of childhood and the compelling rhythms that enable them to be remembered.

> Lucy go lightly
> > Wherever you go,
> Light as a lark
> > From your head to your toe;
>
> In slippers you float
> > And in sandals you flow —
> So Lucy, go lightly
> > Wherever you go.
>
> *Dennis Lee*

Like nursery rhymes, much of contemporary light verse for children just skirts the forbidden and the taboo. Anarchy, titillation, and the risqué counterpoint feeling and sentiment. Word play is a big part of this poetry — puns, tongue twisters, scrambled words, and near-rhyme. Colloquial rhymes, the rhythms of the speaking voice, the storytelling quality, along with the subjects of a child's life, make these new poems accessible to children and introduce poetry as a natural phenomenon, without much pain.

Eve Merriam created *Inner City Mother Goose*, a parody of the rhymes, and not always for children:

One misty moisty morning,
Virus was the weather;
Waiting for the bus to come,
Closed in together.

One began to cough and shake,
Another cursed his mother,
Someone swiped a wallet;
A day like any other.

Of course, poets have always felt the power of Mother Goose. Kate Greenaway's lines from the last century perfectly echo the qualities of the nursery rhymes.

Little wind, blow on the hilltop;
Little wind, blow down the plain;
Little wind, blow up the sunshine;
Little wind, blow off the rain.

Beatrix Potter, an expert on nursery rhymes, brought out two volumes of her own, *Apply Dapply's Nursery Rhymes* and *Cecily Parsley's Nursery Rhymes*. These collections mix some of her own rhymes along with other verses she discovered in the British Museum library. In her own writing, she absorbed some of the latter's smooth rhythms and flowery word play.

Wendy Watson chose two hundred rhymes and organized them within the frame of the cycle of a year and the passing of a day. Her collection, set in a cosy New England village, begins on a frosty January morning and ends on a starry December evening. In between, the rhymes are juxtaposed with the changing seasons and the hour of the day. For example, with the rhyme:

Here am I
Little Jumping Joan
When nobody's with me
I'm always alone

we see a young girl sitting on a rock, skipping rope beside her, looking wistfully in the direction of the rolling Vermont hills. It is late autumn, the colours have faded and in the dim light of late afternoon a few leaves can be seen still clinging to the trees.

Eleanor Farjeon began writing at the turn of the century at the age of six, and her tales and poems are still read by children. The influence of nursery rhymes can be found in the rhythms and cadences of her work.

The banks are rushy green,
    The banks are rushy green,
And steep enough and deep enough to hide a
    Runaway Queen!
Hang your crown in a rush,
Hide your shoes in the bush,
Puddle your feet in the water sweet, you never
    will be seen.
    The banks are rushy green,
    The banks are rushy green,
Put your crown and slippers on, and don't say
    where you've been.

The turn of the century saw the publication of poet Walter de la Mare's *Songs for Childhood* (1902). He admired the old rhymes, and phrases, rhymes, and images from them fill his own work.

"Cherries, ripe cherries!"
    The old woman cried,
In her snowy white apron,
    And basket beside;
And the little boys came,
    Eyes shining, cheeks red,
To buy bags of cherries,
    To eat with their bread.

Mother Goose has been nurturing poets for centuries and she will continue to nudge and tickle today's child poets into inventing their own creations, alongside the rhymes and rhythms they have met along the way.

Mother Goose around the World

Every country has its nursery rhymes for children — lullabies, counting songs, poems about animals, flowers, good and bad children, people who are tall, short, thin, or fat.

For example, this poem has appeared in many countries over the years:

Humpty Dumpty sat on a wall,
Humpty Dumpty had a great fall.
     All the king's horses,
     And all the king's men,
Couldn't put Humpty together again.

In Saxony,

Hümpelken-Pümpelken sat op de Bank,
Hümpelken-Pümpelken fel von de Bank,
Do is ken Dokter in Engelland
De Hümpelken-Pümpelken kurare kann.

And in Denmark,

Lille Trille
Laae paa Hylde;
Lille Trille
Faldt ned af Hylde.
Ingen Mand
I hele Land
Lille Trille curere kan.

Humpty Dumpty even made it into *Alice and Wonderland*. The Opies speculate that the verse may be thousands of years old.

In Demi's collection of traditional Chinese nursery rhymes translated into English, there are poems about the Moon King's silver knife floating over the waves on a quiet night, about the cock crowing at break of day, about dragonflies and fireflies, wild swans and placid green frogs. She says that some of the nursery rhymes in her book were given to her by Tze-Si "Jesse" Huang, who remembered them from his childhood in Wildcat Stream, Chungkin, Szechuan.

The mighty Emperor Ch'in Shih Huang
Built a wall both great and strong;
It was so long and very stout
That it kept the dangerous Tartars out.

Other nursery rhymes and lullabies were collected from the Spanish community in the Americas, passed on from generation to generation by mothers, fathers, and other family members who heard them as children and later sang them to their own children.

Duérmete mi niña,	Sleep, my child,
Duérmete mi sol,	Sleep, my sun,
Duérmete pedazo	Sleep, little piece
De mi corazón	Of my heart.
(*Arrulle al niño para que se duerma.*)	(*Rock the child to sleep.*)

In a very different collection of nursery rhymes by Caribbean poets John Agard and Grace Nichols, we find a fresh alternative to traditional collections. The pair were born and lived in Guyana until 1977, when they moved to Britain, and they look at the familiar nursery rhymes along with a host of entirely original rhymes and characters, including some Caribbean poems drawn from their own childhood memories. Here is one by John Agard:

Pumpkin
Pumpkin
Where have you been?

I been to hallowe'en
to frighten the queen

Pumpkin
Pumpkin
how did you do it?

With two holes for my eyes
and a light
in me head

I frightened the queen
right under her bed!

How suitable are old rhymes for children in multi-ethnic settings? Educator Charles Cornell worries that the traditional Euro-centred heritage of Mother Goose may contain elements that raise obstacles to the academic and social development of young children from other lands and, in some cases, even to children born and raised in our own culture.

> We will have to consider whether language and cultural "monsters" might be lurking within some of them and what we as concerned teachers can do to detect them. Through increased awareness and sensitivity and a reflective attitude toward traditional material, we can avoid some of the communicative and cross-cultural "monsters" that threaten immigrant children, while preserving and providing elements of a rich tradition that will help the children take a unique and productive place in the cultural tapestry that makes society.

A teacher in Columbus, Ohio, told us that last year she discovered a book called *Mary Had a Little Lamb*, and opening the pages noticed that all the nursery rhyme characters were illustrated as African-American. She said that she began to weep, for never had she thought of the nursery rhymes as representing people of colour. This realization touched her deeply, and reminded her of the constant searching she engaged in to find books that included the faces and lives that filled her world. Today we have books for this teacher, her students, and her own children. As well, we must encourage all children to respond to what they hear and read, to challenge the materials, to awaken others in the group to the needs of all, to reinterpret these old words with knowledge we have gleaned along the way, and to bring to the rhymes personal images to sit beside the public views of what these bits of folklore represent.

Based on our own experiences, we feel that nursery rhymes can help children make sense of their own culture, even when far removed from the tradition of the rhymes. We know that children can make friends with young and old in cultures separated by space and time and custom. They can gain a sense of affinity with the family of humankind, creating a positive interest in other customs as opposed to a dislike or fear of strangeness. We can help children examine perceptions, differences, and biases from the safety of literature, comparing, identifying, and participating vicariously in the social language systems of others. The rhymes of old can lead to various cultural responses by members of the class, drawing on their own heritage as they react to and rework these snippets of folklore. The sounds of the English language can roll off the tongue of everyone who joins in the songs and rhymes.

Censoring nursery rhymes isn't a new idea: experts in children's literature note that traditional stories and rhymes have been under attack for years by social reformers who keep trying to adapt traditional tales to suit the morals of the times. But we might question whether rewriting old nursery rhymes is a useful idea. For example, the current *Father Gander* version of "Peter, Peter, Pumpkin Eater" is as follows: Peter "had a wife and wished to keep her", so "he treated her with fair respect, She stayed with him and hugged his neck." As children's literature authority Linda Lamme writes, "If I were to say anything about nursery rhymes, I would say leave them alone. If you want contemporary nursery rhymes, write new ones."

One rhyme was the invention of American Samuel Griswold Goodrich, born in 1793, and an ardent opponent of nursery rhymes. He devoted thirty years to reforming children's literature, almost succeeding in removing nursery rhymes and fairy tales from England and America. "Nursery rhymes," he said, "are nonsense. Anyone, even a child, could make one up. Listen!"

Higglety, pigglety, pop!
The dog has eat the mop;
    The pig's in a hurry,
    The cat's in a flurry —
Higglety, pigglety — pop!

With his rhyme, Goodrich had unwittingly added to the lore of the nursery rhyme, and Maurice Sendak created a book around this nonsense verse. But then, that is the nature of the rhymes themselves — literary bits and pieces passed on for centuries, just for the fun of saying them aloud to children.

We know a two-and-a-half-year-old who is passionate about Mother Goose, especially the version illustrated by Michael Foreman. Attempts to introduce other versions have met with failure. When different examples of the same rhyme are placed side by side with Foreman's, he says "No!" to some and declares, "This is Mother Goose," and points to the Foreman book. Probably he loves the Foreman illustrated version because he was introduced to it first, and it is familiar and predictable. But we also suspect that he finds it funnier and more rambunctious in style than others he has met, and he certainly enjoys a high-spirited oral rendition of the pieces, whether chanted or sung, accompanied by the occasional bounce or hand-clapping. Indeed, it may be that he senses this quality in Foreman's drawings and less so in others.

Part of the fun of exploring a variety of nursery rhyme collections is discovering the ways in which different illustrators have tried to entice the viewer to come and look again at something which is already familiar. With a large body of rhymes to choose from, what lies behind the decisions to select certain ones and, even more interesting, why have they been juxtaposed in a certain fashion? For example, consider the challenge of illustrating:

> When I was a little boy,
> I washed my mammy's dishes;
> I put my finger in my eye
> And pulled out golden fishes.

Any attempt to translate the literal truth into images would be unwelcome at best. To dodge the piece by showing, as some have, a boy staring at the tip of his index finger or a boy bending over and scrubbing a large plate, falls far short of the mark. Perhaps you just leave well enough alone or you follow the lead of the great nineteenth-century illustrator, Randolph Caldecott, and make the piece larger than life, to give it greater meaning. This is precisely what illustrator Dan Jones did with this verse in *Mother Goose Comes to Cable Street*. He drew a boy at a kitchen sink holding a glass plate, then filled the space around him with soap bubbles. One large bubble floats at the boy's eye level and two golden fishes formed from the reflection of an electric light bulb stare out. It is this very ability to suggest that there is more to these verses than meets the eye that distinguishes the great illustrators of Mother Goose from the ordinary ones.

Maurice Sendak has probably been the most exciting visual interpreter of Mother Goose and knows intimately the challenges posed by the body of work. "There is about them a certain baldness that betrays the unwary artist into banalities. The deceptively simple verse seems to just slip out of reach, leaving the illustrator with egg on his face."

Author and artist Arnold Lobel said that he was interested in characters, the quirkier the better. His collection might best be described as a gallery of portraits rather than a series of elaborated stories such as those of Randolph Caldecott or Maurice Sendak. When he began sifting through the vast literature of nursery rhymes, he found an "exuberant and courageous race of human beings". But it was the names and faces that did not conjure up an immediate picture that interested him the most. Their triumphs — and follies — seemed to mirror our own, and he was drawn to them emotionally and artistically: "In a nonsensical way they seem to mirror all of our struggles with the rigors of contemporary living. I decided to focus the attention of my book on these ladies and gentlemen."

The remarkable differences in the subjective responses of artists motivates us to encourage the children to trust their own judgments, not only with nursery rhymes but with all the poetry they will meet. In addition, children can also come to recognize how the oral tradition has been and continues to be mined by contemporary writers and artists.

Educator Stuart Marriott conducted an interesting study of children's choices of illustrators, and the criteria they used for their choices. He asked children to compare the work of eight different nursery rhyme artists, chosen to represent a variety of styles and techniques. He talked to 84 children, 4-year-olds, 7-year-olds, and 10-year-olds in two primary schools, one in London and one in Northern Ireland. Each time he presented a selection of illustrations (for example, of Jack Sprat or Old King Cole) and asked the children to select their favourites.

He used pictures from the following books:

Nicola Bayley's Book of Nursery Rhymes
Little Tommy Tucker; Little Jack Horner; Little Bo Peep; Little Miss Muffet (4 vols) by C. Bracken
The Orchard Book of Nursery Rhymes by Faith Jacques

The Helen Oxenbury Nursery Rhyme Book
Richard Scarry's Best Nursery Rhymes Ever
Mother Goose Comes to Cable Street illustrated by Dan Jones
Over the Moon: A Book of Nursery Rhymes by Charlotte Voake
Mother Goose: A Collection of Nursery Rhymes by Brian Wildsmith

Again and again, the children picked Scarry and Bracken, whose characters are colourful and funny, but whose work sometimes strikes adult critics as literal and sentimental.

We learn from this study that illustrations do matter, that children interact with them in constructive and thoughtful ways. They know what they like and what they dislike, and their opinions may differ from their teachers, parents, and other adult critics. This would be a good study to replicate in your classroom, using pictures from the school collection of nursery rhymes. Would there be variations from class to class, school to school?

Interpretive play is at the heart of the hundreds of illustrated versions of Mother Goose. The artist remembers a rhyme, rereads it, lets images flit across his or her mind, and begins to see the words in time and space. For a long time to come, poems will force artists to reflect and imagine, to crystallize and communicate their musings on the world of Mother Goose, creating anew the characters, the times in which they live, and the events, imagined and real, that fill their lives. The pages will be full of eccentric old people, simple foods, wise parents, talking animals, and topsy-turvy worlds.

Only Mother Goose, that doughty old wonder bird, could have survived the assiduous attention of generations of champions and detractors, illustrators and anthologists. More than merely survive she has positively flourished — younger, fresher, and more superbly beautiful than ever: witness the publication of Mother Goose books of every shape and size that has continued for generations, including the dozens now on the market in America.

Maurice Sendak

With Younger Children

Gina Kolata writes in *The New York Times* that rhyme may train the brain, especially as children focus on the intonation and the matching sounds. In a Yale study, Dr. Sally Shaywitz says we use rhymes to get at the sound structure of words. Dr. Norman Karsnegor at the National Institute of Child Health and Development says that "rhyming may be part of what creates an opportunity for learning language." The Russian writer Kornei Chukovsky says that most children use linking rhythmic pairs of words in their verbal development. The author of *The Language Instinct*, Dr. Steven Pinker, says that rhymes resonate with the way the brain decodes the world. "We like stripes and plaids, we like harmonic sounds, and we like rhymes."

These rhymes long to be said aloud, as they are full of sounds and rhythms. Very young children clap along, sing along, and join in with rhymes that are hundreds of years old, something you remember forever. Humpty Dumpty, Wee Willie Winkie, Little Miss Muffet and the whole colourful cast of characters, along with the rollicking rhymes (to market, to market to buy a fat pig); unforgettable sounds (higglety, pigglety); and gripping stories (sing a song of sixpence) become inextricably bound up in the lives of their listeners.

In what we call 'ear print', the children have the sounds and the words clearly in their ears so that when they meet them in printed form, they have little difficulty reading. As Bill Martin Jr. says, children follow along in their books making sense of the print, so their "eyes can be seeing what their ears are hearing and what their tongues are saying."

When we read rhymes aloud to children, we present them with an enriched language experience, outside their normal linguistic surrounds, and they can make of it what they want. For example, Carol, two-and-a-half years old, is retelling her favourite rhymes:

Umdy Dudty sad on the woll
Umdy Dudty ad a great foll
Aw the king's orses and aw the king's men
Couln but Umdy dogether again
Ay Diddle Diddle an the gat an the fiddle
A gow dump over the moon
A liddle dog laughed to see da bort
And the dis ran away with a boon
[loud burp]
a b c d e f g h i j k l m n o p q r s t u v w x y z
Now I know mine abc
Gome along and zing with me

Dom Dom the biber's son
Dole a big and away woo wa
(*Parent intervenes — "Who's naughty there?"*)
Dom Dom
(*"Why was he naughty?"*)
Begos dat dole a big.

Don Holdoway

In her book *At the Very Edge of the Forest*, Carol Fox highlights the significant contribution made by nursery rhymes and other forms of oral literature in the language development of young children. She cites the power and importance of this material on their imaginative development as well. She writes of Shamima, a six-year-old from Bangladesh, a Sylheti-speaker living in East London, who enjoyed this traditional question-and-answer rhyme.

Where's the mouse?
In her house.
Where's her house?
In the wood.
Where's the wood?
The fire burned it.
Where's the fire?
The water quenched it . . . (and so on).

About three weeks after we had read the poem it was Jahed's birthday. He blew out his birthday candles in morning assembly. Shamima leaned over to me and whispered confidentially: "He quench it, Miss."

With Older Children

Grey goose and gander
Waft your wings together
Carry the king's fair daughter
Across the one strand river

"That's it!" cried Birdy, suddenly remembering what the old woman said to her, and the puzzling words in the song.

"That's what the one strand river is — the one strand river is something you remember forever — the one strand river is whatever you never get over."

Jill Paton Walsh
Birdy and the Ghosties

26

Surprisingly, we enjoy revisiting familiar nursery rhymes with or introducing unknown ones to older children, even in secondary schools. Their hidden stories draw us into unknown caves where we can barely see the centuries of drawings on the walls. Dylan Thomas said that "the best craftsmanship always leaves holes and gaps in the works of the poem so that something that is not in the poem can creep, crawl, flash, or thunder in." The patterns of each discovered language fossil await investigation, and often childhood memories are released in the process. Young people begin to bring meaning to these old verses, to wonder about their origins, the word puzzles, the puns, and to explore the rhythmic power of centuries of patterns. Children can invent and reflect all at once, connecting past memories and present conjectures.

An example of a book that attracts the attention of older children is Maurice Sendak's *We Are All in the Dumps with Jack and Guy*. He creates a dark and troubling picture of society's victims — abandoned children, the homeless, AIDS victims, the impoverished, and the starving. In joining two traditional rhymes from Mother Goose, he interprets them with complex and multi-faceted illustrations, giving young people opportunities for reflecting upon his contemporary creation, and a model for revisiting centuries of childhood.

We are all in the dumps
For diamonds are trumps,
The kittens are gone to St. Paul's!
The baby is bit,
The moon's in a fit.
And the houses are built
Without walls.

Jack and Guy
Went out in the Rye
And they found a little boy
With one black eye.
Come says Jack, Let's
    knock him
On the head.
No says Guy,
Let's buy him some bread.
You'll buy one loaf
And I'll buy two
And we'll bring him up
As other folk do.

Sendak's gift to young people lies in the unstated and unanswered questions that illuminate every page of this book. In reading it, children have no choice but to attempt to bring understanding to the text. They are learning what reading can be as they forage for meaning, in the dust of the print, in the colours of the paintings, and in the sounds of the words.

A grade twelve high school class was given two rhymes to interpret by their teacher. No information was provided, not even the clue that the poems were from Mother Goose. The students' comments reveal much about their past experiences, and about their personal responses to unfamiliar text.

> Old Abram Brown is dead and gone,
> You'll never see him more;
> He used to wear a long brown coat
> That buttoned down before.

- *He was just an ordinary man. There was nothing special about him.*
- *Instead of commenting on a great achievement in the man's life, or on a particular noteworthy characteristic that he may have possessed, the author decides to remember the man by his coat. This might be because the author didn't know anything more about Abram Brown, or maybe there was nothing more significant about Abram Brown's life that was worth commenting on.*
- *It reminded me of how I felt when my great-grandfather passed away. I still remember going over to his apartment with my father and brother and listening to his stories and jokes. Especially his jokes because no matter how many times he told them to me I always forgot the punchline. My great-grandfather was always the one who led our Passover Seders every year. After he died my many relatives stopped paying attention to the service that my grandfather now leads. My great-grandfather kept the spirit of Passover together and joined us all together in prayer, unfortunately he's not here anymore.*
- *The name Abram can be a Biblical reference. The story of Genesis seems to chart the growth of Abram as he gets older and older.*
- *A brown coat that produced a nickname: "Abram Brown".*
- *No matter how old you grow and how long you live, you cannot escape from death.*
- *He appears to be the epitaph of entertainer. I imagine him as being similar to Mel Brooks, or maybe Dr. Seuss, as the words seem very lighthearted.*
- *There is no mourning and no tears, no sweet memories or laughter.*

- *Almost gives me the impression that there is nothing beyond death.*
- *The death did not disturb anyone. The feelings portrayed are neutral and non-committed.*
- *This Abram Brown in the poem could be my neighbour or my brother. I have changed my mind. This is a really deep piece of literature. Wow!*
- *It reminds me of poems I used to write when I was younger and I thought everything had to rhyme.*

How close were the interpretations of the young people? *The Oxford Dictionary of Nursery Rhymes* says, "This nursery rhyme is a relic of a folk-play." In the play *The Mummers*, Father Christmas and two Merrymen carry the character out, singing:

This poor old man is dead and gone,
We shall never see him more,
He used to wear an old grey coat
All buttoned down before.

In a version performed in Hampshire, the name of the man is discovered again:

Oh dear, oh dear, see what I've been and done,
Killed my poor old Father Abraham Brown.

The second rhyme the students responded to was the following:

William and Mary,
    George and Anne,
Four such children
    Had never a man:
They put their father
    To flight and shame,
And called their brother
    A shocking bad name.

- *The length of the poem and its structure relates well to the title. The number four not only represents the number of children, but also is seen through the set-up of the poem. There are four separate statements made, each one rhyming with the previous one.*

- *Perhaps this is a commentary on the existence of cliques and alliances within the family unit.*
- *This poem has an interesting childlike quality to it. It sounds like a nursery rhyme or a song children might sing in a taunting fashion.*
- *I can imagine my teacher Mr. B. learning this song from one of his readers at school and thinking he is very special for knowing it.*
- *The name struck me as very white and upper class, such an unfortunate fate for such privileged pupils.*
- *This poem is reminiscent of Dorothy Parker.*
- *It conveys a simple literal message, but also contains symbolic undertones. Knowing the context would help to understand the poem: e.g., it could be written about a royal family, and therefore have political significance.*
- *It is rather reminiscent of a nursery rhyme.*
- *The author seems to almost tease you with the idea of a tale and then refuses to reveal what happened.*
- *It seems as though it could be in some way representative of England.*
- *People always want to lay all the blame on others when they should really be taking a closer look at themselves.*
- *Is the writer threatening young ones to be good or their paternal unit will leave them?*
- *This poem reinforces children's ideas that they are the cause of divorce and separation.*

The Opies say that this may be a disrespectful rhyme about the daughters and sons-in-law of James II, and their brother, James Francis Edward Stuart, the "Old Pretender." The students were very close to history in their spontaneous understanding of these leftover verses.

Adding the Children's Voices

And what about the cow that jumped over the moon?
In Egypt the sky was always thought of as a cow, her body arching over the earth and her four legs standing firmly upon it.
Again, it is I who make the link not the writer of the rhyme.

P.L. Travers

When young people have opportunities for responding to the

rhymes, they are building literary and literacy powers. They can talk about a poem, read the dialogue aloud, create their own versions, paint, model and role-play characters and events, write about ideas sparked by the poem, or read other poems illustrated by different artists. With the teacher's careful intervention, collaborative responses can extend each child's personal response and help generate a wider and more thoughtful appreciation of the rhymes, and of the nature of print. We want to help children respond to the poems they have listened to or read — not always an easy task. We may begin with a concept — set out art supplies, divide the class into discussion groups, organize an interview in role — but the children will make the meaning, and we as teachers will have to be sensitive to their wants and needs.

In *My Son John* by Jim Aylesworth, this nursery rhme now comes with fourteen new verses in the pattern of the original, and a new cast of characters. Ed, Sue, Neil, Ann, and many others jump out of bed, eat breakfast, milk cows, and go through their day to the same playful rhyme and tumbling rhythm that have made the original Mother Goose verse a favourite.

Yellow yellow sunup,
My son Ed.
Up he jumps
From out of bed.
On go pants
And wool shirt red
Yellow yellow sunup,
My son Ed.

Diddle, diddle, dumpling,
my son John,
Went to bed
with his trousers on;
One shoe off,
and one shoe on,
Diddle, diddle, dumpling,
My son John.

A primary class created their own class poem book, writing similar verses in the pattern, containing their names and some significant points about their interests and possessions.

Some types of poems dictate the work that will follow: controversial endings require talk for clarification; a beautifully illustrated picture book begs for art or media activities. Some groups of children will be hesitant to share unless a sense of trust is created. For each of the rhymes in this book, we offer suggestions for setting up response inquiries, but what follows will be dictated by the energy or the direction each group chooses to follow. We present observations of some classroom experience, but we depend upon your own skills and exploring the learning. Our advice would be to listen to the children, listen to the poem, and listen to your own teaching wisdom.

Walter Crane

1 * WORD PLAY

Tongue Twisters

Mother Goose is all about word play. Words are made up of sounds, rhythms, spellings, and shapes, and this means that they can be played with — arranged, turned around, and repeated. When children play with words, they notice the sounds and rhythms of language and how words work from "inside the language". At recess and on their own, children are constantly fooling with language, from the verses they chant to the jingles and slogans they remember from ads. Of course, children of all ages also need opportunities to observe language and all the bits and pieces that create it. As they laugh at the poems and word play, and puzzle over the way words fit or don't fit, children are developing language expertise. As they experiment with rhyme and rhythm, riddles and tongue twisters, they practice manipulating words and controlling the way words work, growing as language users and in their understanding of how language functions. The unexpected sounds of Mother Goose form the heart of word play.

> Three little ghostesses,
> Sitting on postesses,
> Eating buttered toastesses,
> Greasing their fistesses,
> Up to their wristesses,
> Oh, what beastesses
> To make such feastesses!

This selection and others such as "Robert Rowley", "Moses Supposes", "Three Grey Geese," and "Swan Swam over the Sea" are meant to be spoken aloud quickly, repeatedly, and as accurately as possible. The children can pick one which appeals and learn it by heart. You can hold a contest to determine who can set the record for the most rapid-fire recitations in a row before stumbling, as long as you join in the tongue-twisting.

> Robert Rowley rolled a round roll
>   round,
> A round roll Robert Rowley rolled
>   round;
> Where rolled the round roll
> Robert Rowley rolled round?

> Moses supposes his toeses are roses,
> But Moses supposes erroneously;
> For nobody's toeses are posies of roses
> As Moses supposes his toeses to be.

> Three grey geese in the green grass grazing,
> Grey were the geese, and green was the grazing.

> Swan swam over the sea,
>   Swim, swan, swim!
> Swan swam back again,
>   Well swum swan!

In fifteen-year-old Sarah's poem, the old tongue twister is turned into a striking image of swans in the evening. Transformations allow young writers to begin with one poetic form and slide ideas onto another shape.

SEA SWAN

> Swan flew heavy
> over the sea,
> clapped white wings in the wind:
> snake-neck straight.

> Snow swan
> settled, pressing on the water;
>   watching the faces
> of young girls less white than his feathers.
>   Grey against grey,
> the sea and sky met dull as morning
> upon Wales.

Low in the tide,
    two islands
echoed with hollow bird-cries:
January-bare.

Night-dark, in the hills
Swan swims among the reeds;
neck gold-banded.
Present in dreams;
she calls to her mate.

And at moonset
two swans dawn on the water,
ringed in blue-gold;
part of someone's madness.
Like the swan on our sea,
they unfurl their wings to fly,
    leaving only a ripple on still water.

Riddle Rhymes

Old Mother Twitchett has but one eye,
And a long tail which she can let fly,
And every time she goes over a gap,
She leaves a bit of her tail in a trap.
(Answer: a needle and thread)

Old Mother Twitchett is a riddle which lays down concise clues in an imaginative way. Mother Goose is full of old riddles:

The more you feed it,
The more it'll grow high;
But if you give it water
It'll go and die.
(Answer: fire)

I washed my face in water
That neither rained nor run,
I dried my face on a towel,
That was neither woven nor spun.
(Answer: dew and sun)

My first is in apple and also in pear,
My second's in desperate and also in dare,
My third is in sparrow and also in lark,
My fourth is in cashier and also in clerk,

My fifth is in seven and also in ten,
My whole is a blessing indeed unto men.
(Answer: peace)

Four stiff standers,
Four dilly-danders,
Two lookers,
Two crookers,
And a wig-wag.
(Answer: a cow)

The children can choose a common kitchen gadget or household item (scissors, pencil with an eraser on the end, etc.) and try to disguise it in the form of a riddle poem.

Rhyme Surprises

The following poem is a catalogue of fantastic images.

I saw a peacock with a fiery tail
I saw a blazing comet drop down hail
I saw a cloud with ivy curled around
I saw a sturdy oak creep on the ground
I saw an ant swallow up a whale
I saw a raging sea brim full of ale
I saw a Venice glass sixteen foot deep
I saw a well full of men's tears that weep
I saw their eyes all in a flame of fire
I saw a house high as the moon and higher
I saw the sun at twelve o'clock at night
I saw the man who saw this wondrous sight.

Another version of the same pattern:

I saw a fishpond all on fire
I saw a house bow to a squire
I saw a person twelve feet high
I saw a cottage near the sky
I saw a balloon made of lead
I saw a coffin drop down dead
I saw two sparrows run a race
I saw two horses making lace
I saw a girl just like a cat
I saw a kitten wear a hat

I saw a man who saw these too
And said though strange
    they were all true.

The rhymes can also be read as follows:

I saw a peacock.
With a fiery tail I saw a blazing comet.
Drop down hail I saw a cloud. Etc.

Then the extraordinary images shift dramatically. The children can work with partners to practice speaking the words out loud together, and a few can share their own versions with the class. They can also create a collage using magazine cut-outs to illustrate their own "Wonder of Wonders".

When children innovate on a poem pattern they have enjoyed, they are using their own knowledge of the underlying structures in order to compose. Children borrow their favourite literary structures, expanding their linguistic storehouse, transforming and reshaping the borrowed language and tuning their ears to the beauty of speech. The dependable schemes of rhyme and rhythm help children read words they didn't know they knew.

Short, sharp dialogue is a very effective technique for moving a story along.

Fire! Fire! says Mrs. Dyer;
Where? Where? said Mrs. Dare;
Up the town, said Mrs. Brown.
Any damage? said Mrs. Gamage;
None at all, said Mrs. Hall.

Another nursery rhyme follows the same pattern:

Mrs. Mason broke a bason,
Mrs. Frost asked her how much it cost,
Mrs. Brown said half-a-crown,
Mrs. Flory said what a story.

Margaret Meek reports this children's version:

Mrs. Red went to bed with a turban on her head
Mrs. White had a fright in the middle of the night

Saw a ghost eating toast half-way up a lamp post
Mrs. Brown went to town with her knickers hanging down
Mrs. Green saw the scene and put it in a magazine.

Children can find other examples among the nursery rhymes of events related using short, sharp, stacatto-like dialogue. One of the most successful picture books of recent years, *Yo! Yes!* by Chris Raschka uses this technique in lively exciting fashion. The children can study this book, then attempt to make their own picture books for one of the dialogue pieces they have found.

Julia, who is fifteen, used a series of verbs in a non-rhyming poem to describe a baby's morning meal, and entered the world of Mother Goose.

BABY BREAKFAST

Squidge
My food in my fist
Throw
It at the wall
Rub
It in my hair
Soak
It in my milk
Squeeze
The dirt out
Stuff
It in my mouth
Splurt
It across the room
Dig
It out of my bib
Catapult
It to Mummy
Aim
It at Daddy
Mmmm
Finished.

Children can write short two-line nonsense verses for a class book. They can brainstorm a list of unrelated rhyming words, pairing unusual, humorous words. Perhaps they could use the names of children in the class as a basis for their rhymes.

Alistair Reid loved to play with sounds of language — old

words no longer used, new words which ought to exist. Mother Goose is always around during word play.

It you want to call for silence, say
    MUMBUDGET
If you want to change the subject, say
    PONSONBY
And if someone tells you something you don't believe, look at him steadily and say
    FIRKYDOODLE
    FUDGE
    or
    QUOZ

Silly Stories

What does it mean when people are described as "making small talk"? Is this easy for everyone to do?

As Tommy Snooks and Bessy Brooks
    Were walking out one Sunday,
Says Tommy Snooks to Bessy Brooks,
    "Tomorrow will be Monday."

Children can discuss a question such as this: "Have you ever been in a situation where your thoughts 'dried up' and you said things you felt embarrassed about later?" Together they can create a list of typical "small talk" expressions which they hear every day, and order them in such a way that the effect is like a "found poem".

Old King Cole was a merry old soul,
And a merry old soul was he;
He called for his pipe,
And he called for his bowl,
And he called for his fiddlers three.

And every fiddler had a very fine fiddle,
And a very fine fiddle had he;
Fiddle-diddle-dee went the fiddlers three,
There's none so rare as can compare
With King Cole and his fiddlers three.

The real King Cole ruled Britain in the third century, and possibly the following rhyme refers to him. Old kings in many fairy and folktales are not at all merry. It is often an old king who stands in the way of people's happiness by setting impossible tasks to be accomplished. Children can research in collections of folktales examples of some difficult tasks imposed by a ruler, and arrange the tasks in order of difficulty. Finally, they can report their findings to classmates.

Cock-a-doodle-doo,
My dame has lost her shoe;
My master's lost his fiddling stick
And knows not what to do.

Cock-a-doodle-doo,
What is my dame to do?
Till master finds his fiddling stick.
She'll dance without her shoe.

Cock-a-doodle-doo,
My dame has found her shoe.
And master's found his fiddling stick,
Sing doodle-doodle-doo.

Cock-a-doodle-doo,
My dame will dance with you
While master fiddles his fiddling stick
For dame and doodle-doo.

Pyrotechnics in the barnyard! How do you imitate the cry of a rooster? Is there another expression more effective than cock-a-doodle-doo? Barnyard sound effects pose an interesting challenge for writers. Students can examine picture books about hens, roosters, and other barnyard creatures and compile a list of the best onomatopoeic words they find. Some titles to help you get started are *Gobble Growl Grunt* by Peter Spier, *The Little White Hen* by Pamela Allen, and *Clams Can't Sing* by James Stevenson.

Little Betty Pringle she had a pig,
It was not very little and not very big;
When it was alive it lived in clover,
But now it's dead and that's all over.
Johnny Pringle he sat down and cried,

Betty Pringle she lay down and died;
So there was an end of one, two, three,
Johnny Pringle he, Betty Pringle she,
   And Piggly Wiggly.

Here we have a very different kind of sound, a dirge to be chanted aloud with great solemnity. The fastest way to involve the class is by means of call and response, a line at a time. For example:

Leader: Little Betty Pringle she had a pig
Class: *repeats the line, etc.*

We try to find rhymes to begin with that feature repetitive sequences or refrains which encourage children to join in the fun. Developing a love of the music of words is one of our aims, and providing opportunities to build up a repertoire of pieces we can speak aloud again and again is a priority.

Puss came dancing out of the barn
With a pair of bagpipes under her arm;
She could sing nothing but Fiddle cum, fee
The mouse has married the bumble bee
Pipe, cat — dance, mouse,
We'll have a wedding at our good house.

There are wonderful toe-tapping rhythms which beg to be spoken out loud. Try the above piece as a two-part round while keeping time clapping hands. This rhyme is found in a variety of forms, the earliest recorded appearing to be that in a Wiltshire manuscript dated 1740:

Fiddle-de-dee, fiddle-de-dee!
The wasp has married the bumble bee!
Puss came dancing out of the barn
With a pair of bagpipes under her arm.
One for Johnnie and one for me,
Fiddle-de-dee, fiddle-de-dee!

Another version is as follows:

Fiddle-de-dee, fiddle-de-dee,
The fly shall marry the humble-bee.

They went to the church, and married was she:
The fly has married the humble-bee.

Each of three groups could work with one version and then,
in the sharing, present their poem, followed by a discussion of
the variations. A Scottish one is:

A cat cam fiddlin
Oot o' a barn,
Wi a pair o' bagpipes
Under her arm.

She cud sing naethin but
"Fiddle cum fee,
The moose has mairrit
The bumble bee."

Pipe cat,
Dance moose,
We'll hae a waddin
At oor guid house.

Gerard Benson adopts the literary conceit of bringing the
characters from a rhyme to life. Children may want to describe
what life at their house would be like if one of the rhymes they
enjoy came to life and lived with them.

Once, when I wasn't very big
I made a song about a pig
    Who ate a fig
    And wore a wig
And nimbly danced the Irish jig.

And when I was as small as THAT
I made a verse about a cat
    Who ate a rat
    And wore a hat
And sat (you've guessed) upon the mat.

But yesterday upon my door
I heard a knock; I looked and saw
    A hatted cat
    A wigged pig
    Who chewed a rat
    Who danced the jig
    On my door mat!

They looked at me with faces wise
Out of their bright enquiring eyes,
"May we come in? For we are yours,
Pray do not leave us out of doors.
We are the children of your mind
Let us come in. Be kind. Be kind."

So now upon my fireside mat
There lies a tireless pussy cat
Who all day long chews on a rat
        And wears a hat.

And round him like a whirligig
Dancing a frantic Irish jig
Munching a fig, cavorts a big
        Wig-headed pig.

They eat my cakes and drink my tea.
There's hardly anything for me!
And yet I cannot throw them out
For they are mine without a doubt.

But when I'm at my desk tonight
I'll be more careful what I write.

I'll be more careful what I write.

Randolph Caldecott

2 * VOICES

Bringing the Words to Life

We enjoy working with poems "writ large" displayed on charts or on an overhead projector, and of course big books borrowed from the primary division.

Many features of nursery rhymes can be effectively used in reading aloud.

- monologues, in which the voice that is evident and the unseen audience provide sources for role-playing by the children;
- dialogues, which can act as minimal scripts for the children to interpret, in pairs, in small groups, or as a whole class divided into parts;
- chants, cheers, prayers, invocations, and songs where the children's voices can be raised together as a village, a tribe, a society;
- situations so intense and concentrated that role-playing and improvisation present reading avenues for exploration;

Secondary students in an ESL class were asked to read the following poem aloud in groups several times and then create a story behind the words.

> Here come I,
> Little David Doubt,
> If you don't give me money,
> I'll sweep you all out,
> Money I want,
> And money I crave,
> If you don't give me money,
> I'll sweep you all to the grave.

David Doubt was born in a garbage can. He is 15 years old now. He was born in Russia, he escaped from Russia to America when he was 9 years old. Six years later, he was still escaping countries. Now he lives in Toronto.

His life is terrible. He sleeps in a landfill. He asks for money from people who walk by. If the people don't give him money, he'll throw them into the garbage. He is crazy for money. He's so poor that he didn't have a chance to take a shower for 9 months. Usually he takes one every two months in a little lake close by the landfill, also full of garbage.

I think that this poem can be coming from any place or any country, any place that there is bad government or a place that there are corrupt people in it. In this case David Doubt is a bad person who wants to take some one's money. If this person does not give the money that he wants, David will sweep them to the grave. In other words, he will kill the person. The place can be in any country and the person can be any one and it can happen to any body. For example in Iran the government is very similar to this poem. If you have lots of money or you have a good business some how they will take it from you and if people don't listen to them they will get killed.

Majid Ali

I think that this poem was created for people who love money and for who money is the most important thing in their life. Little David doubt is the person who loves money so much that he is ready to sweep everyone on his way to it and even to kill someone. he was called "Little" by the author because his plans and actions are very horrible, and low for society. If money is more important for him than the life of someone, he is very terrible person and dangerous for society.

Therefore to decrease such situations we have to do something to stop it: as don't let children think that money is the most important thing in their life. There are more beautiful things on the earth than money.

For such people as Little David Doubt we have to have special meetings for them and talk about such problems, and try to explain to them that what they are doing will bring bad influences for society and future generations.

Irina

We can see David is a careless person. He has no love but money. I think what may have made David to become this way is the environment he was living in and the situation he was facing. That is, the difficulty of living without money. He used to be poor and that made him want to be rich. Now he is young and he says this to his parents because he does not know how much it could hurt them.

Although money is important to us and it can buy many things, it cannot buy love and friendship. We shouldn't crave money so but should crave love and friendship so that we will not be lonely.

Kim Luong

O I have been to the meadow-bout fields,
And I have been to the gorses;
And I have been to the meadow-bout fields,
To seek my master's horses.
And I got wet, and very very wet,
And I got wet and weary,
And I was wet, and very very wet
When I came home to Mary!

This is another story which gives only a few clues to the greater story around it. The children can brainstorm a list of questions they would like the speaker of these lines to answer. Then each can work with a partner, one partner being "X"; the other "Y". X is to take the role of the speaker, Y the role of the master whose horses are lost. They can conduct the interview that might take place between the pair.

Some of the best call-and-response stories can be found in nursery rhymes:

Children, children, where have you been?
Granny Grey, we've been to London to visit the Queen.
What did she give you?
A loaf of bread as big as our head,
A piece of cheese as big as our knees.
A lump of jelly as big as our belly.
Where's my share?
Up in the air.
How shall I get it?
Stand on a chair.
What if I fall?
We don't care.

Tough questions are asked frequently by characters in folk-tales as well as in nursery rhymes. In many instances, finding the answer to the tough questions leads to an exciting adventure.

The man in the wilderness asked of me,
how many strawberries grew in the sea?
I answered him, as I thought good,
As many red herrings as grew in the wood.

By asking a series of parallel questions, Mark, aged seven, creates an interesting poetic effect.

Old Man Wind,
Why do you blow the trees to make them shiver?
Why do you whistle in the small gaps?
Why do you roar like a hundred dragons?
Why do you chase the gentle leaves?
Why do you push the small green grass?
Why do you pull my hair?
Go away
Until I want you
To fly my kite.

Jonathan's questions build suspense as the reader begins to imagine the answers.

What's that down there?
What's that moving?
What's that moving down
in the dark?
Is it the monster
Who roars
And kills?
Or is it the skeleton
Who rattles his bones?
What's that down there?
What's that moving?
What's that moving down
in the dark?
Is it a bat?
Flying through the air?
What's that
in the dark?

The celebrated author Russel Hoban uses the question-and-answer form and the rhythm of Mother Goose to create the sense of the ocean.

Old Man Ocean, how do you pound
Smooth glass rough, rough stones round?
    Time and the tide and the wild waves rolling.
    Night and the wind and the long grey dawn.

Old Man Ocean, what do you tell,
What do you sing in the empty shell?
    Fog and the storm and the long bell tolling,
    Bones in the deep and the brave men gone.

Dennis Lee asks a question in one verse and gives the answer in the next.

If I could teach you how to fly
Or bake an elderberry pie
Or turn the sidewalk into stars
Or play new songs on an old guitar
Or if I knew the way to heaven,
The names of night, the taste of seven
And owned them all, to keep or lend —
Would you come and be my friend?

You cannot teach me how to fly.
I love the berries but not the pie.
The sidewalks are for walking on,
And an old guitar has just one song.
The names of night cannot be known,
The way to heaven cannot be shown.
You cannot keep, you cannot lend —
But I still want you for my friend.

The children can read the poem ''The Spiders'' out loud as if one fly were telling it to another fly. Then they can read it as the spiders might. What other ''voices'' for reading might they explore? In groups of three, they can prepare a reading of the piece using three distinct character voices.

At early morn the spiders spin,
And by and by the flies drop in;
And when they call, the spiders say,
Take off your things, and stay all day!

Patterns

Usually, when listening to rhymes containing repetitions and refrains, children will join in automatically. Once they are familiar with the repeated parts, a slight pause by the teller is all that is necessary to invite their response. Nursery rhymes such as the following are excellent sources:

If all the seas were one sea
What a great sea that would be.
If all the trees were one tree
What a great tree that would be.
If all beings were one being
What a great being that would be.
If all the axes were one axe
What a great axe that would be.
And if the great being took the great axe
and chopped down the great tree,
And if the great tree fell into the great sea
What a great SPLASH that would be.

This is the key of the kingdom
In that kingdom is a city,
In that city is a town,
In that town there is a street,
In that street there winds a lane,
In that lane there is a yard,
In that yard there is a house,
In that house there waits a room,
In that room there is a bed,
On that be there is a basket,
    A basket of flowers.

Flowers in the basket,
Flowers on the bed,
Bed in the chamber,
Chamber in the house,
House in the weedy yard,
Yard in the winding lane,
Lane in the broad street,
Street in the high town,
Town in the city,
City in the kingdom:
    This is the key of the kingdom.

Charles Causley's poem "One for the Man" is a good example of a contemporary poem with the shape and feel of the oral tradition.

One for the man who lived by the sand,
Two for his son and daughter,
Three for the sea-birds washed so white
That flew across the water.

Four for the sails that brought the ship
About the headland turning.
Five for the jollyboys in her shrouds,
Six for the sea-lamps burning.

Seven for the sacks of silver and gold
They sailed through the winter weather.
Eight for the places set on shore
When they sat down together.

Nine for the songs they sang night-long,
Ten for the candles shining.
Eleven for the lawmen on the hill
As they all were sweetly dining.

Twelve for the hour that struck as they stood
To the Judge so careful and clever.
Twelve for the years that must come and go
And we shall see them never.

We can speak these words in unison or sing them, or we can begin the piece with one solo voice, then build cumulatively until every child's voice has been included. We can try to determine who is speaking the words to whom and why, then try reading the poem in role. (We have heard this poem performed as a funeral dirge, a pub song with solo voices and chorus, a singing game played by children, a work chant and a marching drill at boot camp.) Certainly the surface of this poem is not the whole story, and once children have explored the text orally in role, many questions support themselves: is this a story of treachery and deceit? Is it a story about pirates? Are the man and his family innocent victims or instigators? Some of these questions can be used to explore the text (students in role as reporters who 'hot seat' the 'judge so careful and clever' to probe his role in the story), or to explore the theme (the children improvise a scene depicting what we associate with pirates of long ago).

For a century the cry "Young lambs to sell" brought children running into the street with their pennies and halfpennies. The toy lambs had white cotton wool fleeces spangled with Dutch gilt, heads of flour paste, horns and legs of tin, and collars of pink tape.

Young lambs to sell! Young lambs to sell!
If I'd as much money as I could tell,
I'd not come here with lambs to sell!
    Dolly and Molly, Richard and Nell,
    Buy my yong lambs and I'll use you will!
            Peter and Iona Opie

In the rhyme,

Tom Tom the Piper's son
Stole a pig and away he run,

children are often concerned about the stolen pig being eaten. The Opies say that modern illustrators depict the scene incorrectly. "The pig was not a live one but a sweetmeat model sold by a street hawker, as is narrated in the chapbooks. 'This man makes pigs of paste and fills their bellies with currants and places two little currants in their heads for eyes.' Vendors of such pigs were common in the eighteenth century. Their street cry is still remembered in some nurseries. . . .' "

The nursery rhymes contain many old cries of street vendors. Children can find examples in other nursery rhyme collections. Are there any "street criers" left in our country? What examples can the children provide? They might interview senior citizens in their community about street criers they may remember. Their findings could be pooled for an oral performance, a soundscape of street cries that might have been heard in their community a hundred years ago.

Get ready your money and come to me,
I sell a young lamb for one penny.
Young lambs to sell! Young lambs to sell!
If I'd as much money as I could tell,
I never would cry, Young lambs to sell!

Here's Finiky Hawkes,
    As busy as any;

Will well black your shoes,
　　And charge but a penny.

If I'd as much money as I could spend,
I never would cry, Old chairs to mend.
Old chairs to mend! Old chairs to mend!
I never would cry, Old chairs to mend.

Here I am with my rabbits
　　Hanging on my pole,
The finest Hampshire rabbits
　　That e'er crept from a hole.

Here's a large one for the lady,
Here's a small one for the baby;
Come buy, my pretty lady,
Come buy o'me a broom.

John Agard adds his own Caribbean street cries, and ESL students may know cries from their native lands, all of which can be translated and compared with each other.

Songs

Nursery rhymes that are also songs can be spoken and then sung, so that the children can discover how mood shifts dramatically from words spoken to words sung. "The Lover's Gifts" below is one example.

My love sent me a chicken without e'er a bone;
He sent me a cherry without e'er a stone;
He sent me a Bible that no man could read;
He sent me a blanket without e'er a thread.

How can there be a chicken without e'er a bone?
How can there be a cherry without e'er a stone?
How can there be a Bible that no man can read?
How can there be a blanket without e'er a thread?

When the chicken's in the eggshell, there is no bone;
When the cherry's in the blossom, there is no stone;
When the Bible's in the press, no man can it read;
When the wool is on the sheep's back, there is no thread.

This Little Puffin, compiled by Elizabeth Matterson, is a good source for words and music, as are Jane Yolen's *Mother Goose Song Book* and Charles Causley's contemporary 'nursery rhyme' poetry in *Early in the Morning*.

Another rhyme that tells a story of lovers may be more familiar to some readers. It can also be sung.

Can you make me a cambric shirt,
    Parsley, sage, rosemary, and thyme,
Without any seam or needlework?
    And you shall be a true lover of mine.

Can you wash it in yonder well,
    Parsley, sage, rosemary, and thyme,
Where never sprung water, nor rain ever fell
    And you shall be a true lover of mine.

Can you dry it on yonder thorn,
    Parsley, sage, rosemary, and thyme,
Which never bore blossom since Adam was born
    And you shall be a true lover of mine.

Now you've asked me questions three,
    Parsley, sage, rosemary, and thyme,
I hope you'll answer as many for me,
    And you shall be a true lover of mine.

Can you find me an acre of land,
    Parsley, sage, rosemary, and thyme,
Between the salt water and the sea sand?
    And you shall be a true lover of mine.

Can you plough it with a ram's horn,
    Parsley, sage, rosemary, and thyme,
And sow it all over with one peppercorn?
    And you shall be a true lover of mine.

Can you reap it with a sickle of leather,
    Parsley, sage, rosemary, and thyme,
And bind it up with a peacock's feather?
    And you shall be a true lover of mine.

When you have done and finished your work
    Parsley, sage, rosemary, and thyme,
Then come to me for your cambric shirt,
    And you shall be a true lover of mine.

The nursery rhyme "Billy, My Son" preserves in short and simple form what is perhaps the last living (i.e., still orally transmitted) link with a tale possibly terrible in origin and certainly mysterious in its subsequent history. The lines are descended from the ballad "Lord Randal", which has been found as far east as Czechoslovakia and Hungary, as far north as Sweden and Iceland, and as far south as Calabria.

Where have you been today, Billy, my son?
Where have you been today, my only man?
I've been a-wooing, mother, make my bed soon,
For I'm sick at heart; and fain would lay down.

What have you ate today, Billy, my son?
What have you ate today, my only man?
I've ate eel-pie, mother, make my bed soon,
For I'm sick at heart, and shall die before noon.

Choral Dramatization

In choral dramatizations, the children explore the sounds and rhythms of language as they interpret poems, songs, and chants. Many children need an extra incentive to enjoy the experience of choral reading; dramatization of the selection can provide this, helping the children feel the music and meaning of the words. Selections with the strongest appeal for the children will probably be those that enable them to form clear images of what the words are saying. As children gain experience, they may interpret more complex selections, using sound and movement, or creating still pictures as a narrator reads the selection.

What are you doing, my lady, my lady,
What are you doing, my lady?

I'm spinning old breeches, good body, good body,
I'm spinning old breeches, good body.

Long may you wear them, my lady, my lady,
Long may you wear them, my lady.

I'll wear 'em and tear 'em, good body, good body,
I'll wear 'em and tear 'em, good body.

I was sweeping my room, my lady, my lady,
I was sweeping my room, my lady.

The cleaner you'd be, good body, good body,
The cleaner you'd be, good body.

I found me a sixpence, my lady, my lady,
I found me a sixpence, my lady.

The richer you were, good body, good body,
The richer you were, good body.

I went to the market, my lady, my lady,
I went to the market, my lady.

The further you went, good body, good body,
The further you went, good body.

I bought me a pudding, my lady, my lady,
I bought me a pudding, my lady.

The more meat you had, good body, good body,
The more meat you had, good body.

I put it in the window to cool, my lady,
I put it in the window to cool.

The faster you'd eat it, good body, good body,
The faster you'd eat it, good body.

The cat came and ate it, my lady, my lady,
The cat came and ate it, my lady.

And I'll eat you too, good body, good body,
And I'll eat you too, good body.

In "Six Little Mice Sat Down to Spin," the class can develop the selection for choral speaking, possibly using one or two narrators and solo voices for the cat and the mice. They can research other stories from folklore in which a powerful figure wants in at a door and smaller, less powerful characters must outwit the would-be intruder.

Six little mice sat down to spin;
Pussy passed by and she peeped in.
What are you doing, my little men?
Weaving coats for gentlemen.
Shall I come in and cut off your threads?
No, no, Mistress Pussy, you'd bite off our heads.
Oh, no, I'll not; I'll help you to spin.
That may be so, but you can't come in.
Says Puss: You look so wondrous wise,

I like your whiskers and bright black eyes;
Your house is the nicest house I see,
I think there is room for you and for me.
The mice were so pleased that they opened the door,
And Pussy soon had them all dead on the floor.

The children can brainstorm a list of "sound words" to describe
a fight between two cats including invented words like PSSFFT!
They can practice their sound words out loud, experimenting with
loud/soft, fast/slow, high or low pitch sounds.

There once were two cats of Kilkenny,
Each thought there was one cat too many,
So they fought and they fit,
And they scratched and they bit,
Till excepting their nails,
And the tips of their tails,
Instead of two cats, there weren't any.

The children can work in groups to prepare a reading which
incorporates some of the sound words along with the text. They
might like to tape-record their readings.

E.M. Simon

3 ✱ POEM PATTERNS

ABCs

A was an archer, who shot at a frog,
B was a butcher, and had a great dog,
C was a captain, all covered with lace,
D was a drunkard, and had a red face.
E was an esquire, with pride on his brow,
F was a farmer, and followed the plough,
G was a gamester, who had but ill-luck,
H was a hunter, and hunted a duck,
I was an innkeeper, who loved to carouse,
J was a joiner, and built up a house.
K was King William, once governed this land,
L was a lady, who had a white hand.
M was a miser, and hoarded up gold,
N was a nobleman, gallant and bold.
O was an oyster girl, and went about town,
P was a parson, and wore a black gown.
Q was a queen, and wore a silk slip,
R was a robber, and wanted a whip.
S was a sailor, and spent all he got,
T was a tinker, and mended a pot.
U was a usurer, a miserable elf,
V was a vintner, who drank all himself.
W was a watchman, and guarded the door,
X was expensive, and so became poor.
Y was a youth, that did not love school,
Z was a zany, a poor harmless fool.

Mother Goose rhymes were among the earliest to appear in books published for children, to teach the young their letters and provide them with moral instruction according to the cultural norms of their time and place. Today alphabet books, which are available in large numbers and a wide variety of subject and style, serve to provide children of all ages with much to look at, to think about and, when shared with an adult, to talk about. Alphabet books may be used to help children identify familiar objects, as well as letters and sounds; to understand and organize graphic experiences, and to develop their observational and discussion skills. Older children can reinterpret the rhymes and create new versions, illustrating them for peers or younger buddies.

In America, the above rhyme was printed in Boston as early as 1761. In the first half of the nineteenth century several alphabets began "A was an archer", but there was a couplet for each letter:

A was an Archer and shot at a frog,
But missing his mark shot into a bog . . .

The care artists take in the graphic design of children's books — how much goes on a page, the size of the print — is equally important for classroom publishing. When children write their own work, they should be able to read it easily.

The children in Jo Phenix's class brainstormed to find rhymes for each letter and create a pattern book based on the nursery rhyme "A was an Apple Pie". The brainstorming of the story line was done as a group, and individual children then chose pages to illustrate.

A was an airplane.
B built it.
C cleaned it.
D dusted it.
E entered it.
F flew it.
G gassed it up.
H heard it take off.
I iced up the wings.
J just landed it.
K kept the key.
L looped the loop.
M made the engine.
N named it.
O opened the door.

P piloted it.
Q quit the job.
R rode in it.
S stopped it.
T towed it.
U unfastened the seat-belt.
V vacuumed it.
W watched the movie.
X exited.
Y yawned on it.
Z zoomed into the air.

An interesting point about alphabet books is that children can do a lot of research using ABC books in the classroom. They don't know many words beginning with Q, and they find it interesting to make a list and decide which one they can use in their story. Then they start looking for words they can use for X and other more difficult letters. Here they were starting from a book called *Q Is for Duck*. It didn't take the children long to catch on to the pattern.

A is for trampoline.   Why? Because the trampoline has acrobats.
B is for house.   Why? Because a house is built.
C is for baby.   Why? Because a baby cries.
D is for fire.   Why? Because a dragon breathes fire.
E is for volcano.   Why? Because a volcano erupts.

The answers are written upside down, and it's interesting to watch which children bother to turn the page and which ones just go ahead and read upside down. This exercise requires much more thought. The children are really fooling with the language, working with the concept, and building a whole new pattern.

Numbers

One, two,
Buckle my shoe;
Three, four,
Knock at the door;
Five, six,
Pick up sticks;
Seven, eight,

Lay them straight;
Nine, ten,
A big fat hen.
Eleven, twelve,
Dig and delve;
Thirteen, fourteen,
maids a-courting;
Fifteen, sixteen,
Maids in the kitchen;
Seventeen, eighteen,
Maids in waiting;
Nineteen, twenty,
My plate's empty.

Counting books, like alphabet books, come in endless types, forms, and styles. They range from those that present numbers in the simplest manner, to those whose contents are related by theme or tale, to those that serve as vehicles for aesthetic experiences of various kinds rather than as concept books. Counting books are, of course, no substitute for the young child's touching, playing with, and manipulating real objects in order to learn basic mathematical concepts such as number sequence, one-to-one correspondence, grouping, place value, and sets. But counting books are a vital complement to these activities, and nursery rhymes have been part of the counting experience for centuries.

One's lucky,
Two's unlucky,
Three is health,
Four is wealth,
Five is sickness
And six is death.

Once, twice, thrice,
I give thee warning,
Please to make pancakes
'Gin tomorrow morning.

One I love, two I love,
Three I love, I say,
Four I love with all my heart,
Five I cast away;

Six he loves, seven she loves, eight both love.
  Nine he comes, ten he tarries,
Eleven he courts, twelve he marries.

There were two wrens upon a tree,
Whistle and I'll come to thee;
Another came, and there were three,
Whistle and I'll come to thee;
Another came and there were four,
You needn't whistle any more,
For being frightened, off they flew,
And there are none to show to you.

The counting verse below is patterned on "One, One, Cinnamon Bun" by Clyde Watson. The teacher, Jo Phenix, printed the students' ideas for the counting rhyme on chart paper, and they used this as material for choral reading. Here, the oral words came before the writing; the children did the illustrations for the story and published it in a book, *One, One, Elephants Come*.

One, one, elephants come,
two, two, kangaroo,
three, three, honeybee,
four, four, lions roar,
five, five, sea lions dive,
six, six, baby chicks,
seven, seven, a bear called Kevin,
eight, eight, monkeys wait,
nine, nine, porcupine,
ten, ten, start again.

Using the number pattern, Michael Rosen sticks with "one" for his poem. Could each child or group work with only one number to build a poem?

one bloke
one Suzuki
one cylinder
one spark plug
one journey
one a.m.
thousands driven crazeeeeee

The poet Paul Janeczko wrote a take-off on Mother Goose's counting poem, and brought it into this century.

Ten little aliens landed feeling fine
One bought a hot tub and then there were nine

Nine little aliens stayed up very late
One overslept and then there were eight.

Eight little aliens took the name of Kevin
One died laughing and then there were seven.

Seven little aliens studied magic tricks
One disappeared and then there were six.

Six little aliens learned how to drive
One missed the exit and then there were five.

Five little aliens polished the floor
One slipped and fell and then there were four.

Four little aliens visited the zoo
One liked the ape and then there were two.

Two little aliens baked in the sun
One got well-done and then there was one.

One little alien went looking for fun
He never came back and now there are none.

"Thirty days Hath September" is perhaps the best known mnemonic rhyme in the English language. Can the children find other examples of mnemonic verse in their own communities? (A few years ago, the post office encouraged everyone to create mnemonics for the newly implemented postal codes. Perhaps examples of these can be collected or the students can make postal code mnemonics for themselves.)

Weekday Rhymes

The following verse might possibly have been devised to help children learn the days of the week. Cultural patterns (days of the week, months of the year, etc.) are common in the traditional nursery verses. The children can collect examples of cultural patterns used by modern poets.

Solomon Grundy
Born on a Monday
Christened on Tuesday,
Married on Wednesday,
Took ill on Thursday,
Worse on Friday,
Died on Saturday,
Buried on Sunday.
This is the end of Solomon Grundy.

James, aged eleven, uses the weekday pattern to build his "worry"
poem, offering children a model for listing their own weekly concerns.

I worry a lot
Boy do I worry
On Mondays I worry
On Tuesdays I worry
On every day of the week
I worry
I worry about anything
and everything.

I'd like to be someone
who doesn't worry
Boy do I wish I didn't
worry
Here I go again worrying
about worrying
I wish I didn't worry about
worrying about worrying.

Kate Greenaway

4 * GAMES AND RITUALS

For younger children, the charms of games, counting-out rhymes, rituals, and chants probably lie in the simple words and the mesmerizing repetition. Later, the appeal will be in the tricks of language which the rhymes offer.

According to Alison Lurie:

> Children today play games that are known in tribal Africa and were familiar in ancient Rome. When a child climbs a pile of stones and shouts "I'm the king of the castle, get down you dirty rascal!" he is repeating a Roman citizen's taunt; when an older boy or girl shows a baby the "two little birds sitting on a hill, one named Jack and the other named Jill," she or he is rehearsing a nursery entertainment known on four continents.

Just as children's oral traditions (games, rhymes, riddles, jokes) have connections in history, archaeology, anthropology, literature, popular culture, and art, so too do nursery rhymes.

> Hickory Dickory Dock
> The mouse ran up the clock
> the clock struck one
> and down he ran
> Hickory Dickory Dock

"Hickory Dickory Dock," undoubtedly one of the more familiar nursery rhymes with contemporary children was, according to Andrew Lang, part of children's ritual play. "Hickory Dickory Dock is a rhyme for counting out a lot for children. The children on whom the last word falls has to run after the others in a game of 'Tig'."

Circle games (Ring-a-ring o' roses), line games (Red rover), winding games (How many miles to Babylon), hand games (What's in there/gold and money), and remnants of many others are contained in the verses of Mother Goose. Over time, verses have been forgotten, actions dropped, and mime and movement sequences abandoned. Some of these games can be taught to the children using such helpful sources as *Step It Down* by Bessie Jones and Bes Lomax Hawes, but the children can also be encouraged to supply some of the elements from their own games of playground and neighbourhood to bring the words of the verses to life. In fact, their own movement and singing inventions may prove fertile ground for incorporating the rhymes of Mother Goose.

Conversations give children the experience of both the teller and the told. In addition, they encourage speculation about the larger story that the words suggest. Iona and Peter Opie's *Children's Games in Street and Playground* and *The Singing Game* open up a world of possibilities for ritual enactment of some of these conversation pieces. In playing out "How Many Miles to Babylon", for example, the children reveal possible layers of meaning (what is the urgency in arriving before candlelight? How are the possible dangers of arriving late suggested by the way the game is played?).

> How many miles to Babylon?
> Three score miles and ten.
> Can I get there by candlelight?
>
> Yes and back again.
> If your heels are nimble and light
> You may get there by candlelight.

Clyde Watson is an expert at reinterpreting Mother Goose. His word choice, phrasing, and content are so magical that the children may have difficulty realizing he wrote them:

> How many miles to Newburyport
> For trinkets and sweets of every sort?
>   One, two, three, four,
>   Only one mile more.
>
> How many miles to Lavender Spring
> To hear a fine trumpeter play for the King?

One, two, three, four,
Here we are, we'll go no more.

Other rhymes act out rituals. The one that follows might be used to determine who gets first turn at whatever activity follows the choosing ritual.

Whit's in there?
Gowd an money.
Whaur's my share o't?
The moosie ran awa wi't.
Whaur's the moosie?
In her hoosie.
Whaur's her hoosie?
In the wid.
Whaur's the wid?
The fire burnt it.
Whaur's the fire?
The watter quencht it.
Whaur's the water?
The broon bull drank it.
Whaur's the broon bull?
Back o'Burnie's Hill.
Whaur's Burnie's Hill?
A' claid wi snaw.
Whaur's the snaw?
The sun meltit it.
Whaur's the sun?
Heigh, heigh up i the air.

A pole or long stick could be tossed up and the catcher would say the line "Whit's in there?" The opposite player would place his or her hand next to the catcher's on the pole and say "Gowd an money". The rhyme continues in call-and-response fashion while hand over hand the top of the pole is reached. Last hand to fit the pole wins.

It is accepted by many people that this little jingle which our youngsters chant so joyfully had gruesome beginnings.

Ring-a-ring o' roses,
A pocket full of posies;
Atishoo, atishoo, we all fall down.

It seems likely that it was a skit on the Great Plague which hit Britain in approximately 1664. The "ring-a-roses" was the mark on the skin that was a symptom of the dreaded disease. The "pocket full of posies" were the "magic" herbs that were carried in the pocket to ward off the virus. "Atishoo, atishoo" referred to a cold, which was also one of the symptoms, and "we all fall down" meant that the person had either collapsed or was dead!

Herbs were in much demand, and street vendors provided many varieties, used for medical potions or as lucky charms to ward off disease — hence the proverbial "pocket full of posies".

Who'll buy my lavender, fresh lavender,
Sweet blooming lavender, who'll buy?

Iona and Peter Opie have linked games played in school playgrounds with ancient pagan customs. London Bridge would be a good example, tying in the ancient custom of burying human remains at the gates of city walls with the line in the rhyme "here comes a chopper to chop off your head."

Some nursery rhymes are complete dramas which children can enact. "Old Roger Is Dead and Laid in His Grave" is one example which we have seen played.

Old Roger is dead and laid in his grave,
Laid in his grave, laid in his grave;
Old Roger is dead and laid in his grave,
H'm ha! laid in his grave.

Children join hands in a circle and revolve around a child (Old Roger), covered by sweaters and coats who lies in the centre of the circle.

They planted an apple tree over his head,
Over his head, over his head;
They planted an apple tree over his head,
H'm ha! over his head.

Children, still holding hands, advance towards Old Roger and lift their arms over their heads, as close to the body as possible, then retreat.

The apples grew ripe and ready to fall,
Ready to fall, ready to fall;
The apples grew ripe and ready to fall
H'm ha! ready to fall.

Children circle Old Roger in opposite directions, still linked.

There came an old woman a-picking
   them all,
A picking them all, a-picking them all;
There came an old woman a-picking
   them all,
H'm ha! picking them all.

Children drop hands and mime collecting apples.

Old Roger jumps up and gives her a
   knock,
Gives her a knock, gives her a knock;
Which makes the old woman go
   hippety-hop
H'm ha! hippety-hop.

Children continue apple picking but must from time to time go as close to Old Roger as possible. At some point, Old Roger leaps out from the pile of sweaters and coats and chases the players. The one tagged now becomes Old Roger.

Walter de la Mare uses the game of hide and seek to describe the arrival of sleep, and children could use any game they know as a metaphor or analogy in a poem.

Hide and seek, says the Wind,
   In the shade of the woods;
Hide and seek, says the Moon,
   To the hazel buds;
Hide and seek, says the Cloud,
   Star on to star;
Hide and seek, says the Wave
   At the harbour bar;
Hide and seek, says I,
   To myself, and step
Out of the dream of Wake
   Into the dream of Sleep.

The following nursery rhyme remnants could be the beginnings of a new series of games the children invent or adapt.

Draw a pail of water
    For my lady's daughter;
My father's a king, and my mother's a queen,
My two little sisters are dressed in green,
Stamping grass and parsley,
    Marigold leaves and daisies.
One-a-me rush! Two-a-me rush!
Pray thee, young lady, creep under the bush.

Hinx, minx, the old witch winks,
The fat begins to fry,
Nobody at home but Jumping Joan,
Father, Mother and I,
Stick, stock, stone dead,
Blind men can't see,
Every knave will have a slave,
You or I must be he.

Rosy apple, lemon and a pear
A bunch of roses shall she wear
A sword and a pistol by her side,
She shall be a bride.
Take her by the lily-white hand
Lead her across the water,
Blow a kiss and say goodbye —
She's the captain's daughter.

Arthur Rackham

5 * STORIES FROM THE RHYMES

Constructing the stories hidden within the rhymes offers a powerful dynamic for learning. The discussion about the rhyme can be spontaneous or directed by the teacher, and the children can put forward their own concerns. They can use story talk as the starting point for projects of all kinds — research, role-playing, writing, storytelling, reading aloud, painting. By beginning with story talk, the teacher allows all the areas of concern to the children to be brought into the open, so that they can begin making meaning, both personal and collective, using the medium of talk — invisible print that can be edited and reformed so easily — to understand the depth of the printed story rhyme.

Story talk with the whole class is an effective use of the talk mode, but it presents some difficulties. The number of children who can respond during the session is limited by time, opportunity, the ability of each child to speak aloud in large groups, and the group's ability to listen and respond sensitively and meaningfully. As well, it may be difficult to hear everyone unless the furniture is rearranged. However, story talk with the whole class presents a public forum for shared common experiences related to story. It can allow for reflective talk after other response modes have been explored. Children can talk about the pictorial representations, the writing, the drama, the research, etc. The talk may focus on the story meanings or on the storyteller, on the children's identification with the story, on the stories within the story, on the background information, on the conflict, the resolution, the use of language, the difficulty of idiom, the word choice, the sentence structure, the style. It is important that the story talk at times be focused on the story rhyme itself, whether at the beginning of story talk, or as a summary or reflection of the dialogue that has taken place. The children may leave the story in order to understand it better, but they should return to see its reflection in the new learning, the new meaning that has grown from the talk.

Writer Alison Lurie uses the words "economical" and "indirect" to describe many of the rhymes of Mother Goose. So many of the nursery rhymes merely hint at stories, causing them to haunt our imaginations. While many nursery rhymes can be read right through for their stories, others demand a slower, closer reading, and only when we give free rein to our curiosity and imagination does the bigger story begin to emerge.

> Bessy Bell and Mary Gray
>> They were two bonnie lassies:
> They built their house upon the lea
>> And covered it with rushes.
>
> Bessy kept the garden gate,
>> And Mary kept the pantry;
> Bessy always had to wait,
>> While Mary lived in plenty.

This rhyme raises many questions:

- Why did two attractive young women (bonnie lassies) choose to take up residence in a remote area (upon the lea)?
- Why were they living in such makeshift circumstances (covered it with rushes)?
- What was their relationship — friends, cousins, co-workers?
- Why was a well-to-do person living this way (Mary lived in plenty)?
- Did Bessie have any choice in this matter (Bessie had to wait)?
- Were the two women fleeing from difficult circumstances (love affair gone awry; natural disaster; war; escape from someone)?
- Does the story have a happy ending?

Here is a rhyme chock a block with possible meanings and, as with so many of Mother Goose's tightly packed and condensed stories, the reader can wander around inside and outside, making the story whatever he or she wants it to be. The story of Bessy Bell and Mary Gray, however, may be a true story and the nursery rhyme an elliptical version of an old Scottish ballad. It appears two women were indeed friends, and it was while Bessy was visiting Mary (about 1645) that the Plague broke out in Perth, seven miles away from Mary's village. In order to escape it, the two women fled to what they hoped was safer ground. Eventually, they caught the Plague from the young man who brought them their provisions and who was also in love with them, and they died. Approximately 3,000 people are thought to have fallen to the Plague in that region and it is likely that the two women were already infected when they fled. Nursery rhymes contain many powerful examples of individuals fleeing from terrible creatures or catastropic events.

Strange Sightings

Nursery rhymes contain some of the best "moon lore" and images of flight in the oral tradition. Whether the moon is being jumped over, used as a clothes dryer ("Scrabble Hill"), or a place to escape to ("On Saturday Night"), stories abound.

Students can collect examples and catalogue the kinds of flying apparatus used in the poems. There will be several, like "Flying-Man," which give no clues about how the individual performs the feat. The students could design some "Mother Goose" flying machines or devices which might do the job. A connecting story to read together about a "Flying-Man" is *Wingman* by Manus Pinkwater.

Children might consider creating a themed analogy of moon verse selected from the nursery rhymes with accompanying drawings which try to capture the many facets of "moon people" which are presented.

"Flying-man, Flying-man,
Up in the sky,
Where are you going to,
Flying so high?"

"Over the mountains,
And over the sea."
"Flying-man, Flying-man,
Can't you take me."

The points below emerged in a discussion with Shahlena and Casey, nine-year-olds who had read "Flying-Man".

It could be

- *Superman or a bird.*
- *Maybe it means a long distance.*
- *Are they going up north?*
- *Or going on holiday?*
- *Maybe a person who wants to fly is telling another animal who can't fly (an ant, rabbit) that if it flies, people can't kill it.*
- *I think it's a man with magic powers that is flying,*
- *Yeah, a man with wings.*
- *Flying so high can't hit mountains or buildings.*
- *He might be trying to get away from something like the police.*
- *Maybe Flying-Man is a good guy, but maybe not.*
- *He's wearing a cape, and could even be a superbird.*
- *I think that a person is thinking this poem, but Flying-Man can't hear it.*
- *It sounds like they're sitting and thinking about Flying-Man.*
- *Maybe they are sitting on a mountain or in a forest, or on a boat. They can climb on the mast of a boat to see the Flying-Man.*
- *Perhaps the Flying-Man wants to escape from prison and hide in the mountains.*

Shahlena wrote a poem in her journal at the end of the discussion:

Oh I wish I was
So clever as you
To make such a thing
To fly away in
Like you.

Building a Character

There was an old woman tossed up in a basket
Nineteen times as high as the moon;
Where she was going I couldn't but ask it,
For in her hand she carried a broom.

"Old Woman, old woman, old woman," said I,
"O whither, O whither, O whither, so high?"

"To brush the cobwebs off the sky!
And I'll be back again by and by."

Children can read this poem chorally, in unison, line by line, or in reader's theatre fashion with narrator and solos. Then, in groups of four, they may pretend that the old woman lives in their neighbourhood, and they may create imaginary memories about her and take turns relating these memories.

One class created a play using the following outline:

Scene 1
In pairs as A and B, A is a neighbour of the old woman. B is a journalist doing a background feature on the old woman. B interviews A.

Scene 2
A is a police officer. B is the old woman.
A charge of public mischief is being brought against B for participating in a dangerous stunt. B must defend her actions. In groups of four, the children can prepare the old woman's defense, helping to plan a strategy to free her. The teacher can work in role as the judge. Each lawyer gets a turn to appeal to the judge. Advisors may be consulted if a lawyer needs help answering the judge's queries.

Another group of primary children held a story discussion about the meaning of this rhyme, and parts of the transcribed talk are as follows:

1: *She's a witch because she has a broom.*
Teacher: *Was the basket floating?*
2: *No, she was tossed.*
3: *But she kept on going when she got so high. She couldn't stop.*
1: *How did she stop?*
2: *She couldn't.*
3: *The guy singing to her could be a wizard.*
Teacher: *Why do you think it's a wizard?*
3: *That's the only one who could toss her.*
1: *Or a witch.*
Teacher: *"Nineteen times . . ." Michael — it's an exaggeration.*
3: *But a wiz could toss her over the moon.*

5: "To brush the cobwebs. . ."
Teacher: Do you think she's brushing cobwebs?
1: There are no spiders in the sky.
Teacher: So what is she brushing?
3: Stars.
1: The Milky Way.
3: She could be imagining all this in her house and she has to brush up the cobwebs off the ceiling.
1: Exaggeration — she could be saying that the cobwebs are as high as the moon.
6: Did she wipe the cobwebs off before? "And I'll be back. . ."
3: Ya! She's done it before.
3: Maybe she thinks it's not fun doing this so she needs to make it fun by using her imagination.
3: Ya, she's imagining that she's wiping the stars.
1: She's making it more fun.
4: But if she's in her house, who is talking to her?
3: Her cat or her husband.
6: But do cats talk?
3: It's a black cat, a magic cat.
1: The cat is a magic cat. The woman is an ordinary woman.
6: But what about the basket?
Teacher: Was she sitting in the basket?
1: Ya.
Teacher: Who tossed her? How come he doesn't know where she is going?
3: We have to find out who's saying that.
1: Maybe it's a song that she's singing while she's cleaning.
3: The old woman is Mother Goose and she's trying to invent another song or poem while she's doing her work.
3: She's going up on a ladder with a broom and a basket.
Teacher: Cobwebs in the mind.
4: Cobwebs in her mind?
Teacher: Things not clear in her mind.
3: She can think better when her house is not dirty.
1: It gets on her nerves because she can't move around a lot and she can't think clearly.

Other children created pictures based on their visions of the old woman.

There was an old woman

I laughed. It was funny.

The book was good

There was a maid on Scrabble Hill,
And if not dead, she lives there still.
She grew so tall, she reached the sky,
And on the moon hung clothes to dry.

Working with this poem, the children attempted to come to grips with the maid's height:

- *so tall she thought others would make fun of her so she moved away by herself to a castle far away from the city*
- *used to be a maid*
- *went to castle and kicked the people out*
- *when she got there, she was small but then grew*
- *ate radioactive vegetables (and every once in a while she would grow tall and then go back to normal size; but when she got to the castle she got big again and stayed tall (all her food finally digested)*
- *she lives in the castle, but has to crawl (it's the only thing big enough for her to live in)*
- *she was a maid for a family of rich people*
- *her work was getting too slow so they tricked her into eating these vegetables so then she would have to leave*
- *they got back the maid that they used to have*

The man in the moon
Came down too soon
And asked his way to Norwich
He went by the south
And burnt his mouth
From supping cold plum porridge.

In the nineteenth century, the "man in the moon" used to negotiate bribes at election time, but this poem was found earlier. It may date from the time before modern cloth converted plum porridge into plum pudding.

What is the bigger story here? Why was he in such a hurry to reach earth? Was he pushed or did he tumble deliberately? Why was he looking for Norwich? Was he going to a secret meeting? Did someone lure him to earth to kidnap him? How can you burn yourself on something cold? What other difficulties did the man in the moon experience when he came to earth? How did his being the "moon man" contribute to those difficulties?)

We encourage the children not only to question the text but to devise ways of reading the lines out loud so that some of these questions can be answered, just by the manner in which we speak the words. The simple challenge to the children is: "Who is telling the story to whom and why?" In a speech in Toronto, detective writer P.D. James revealed that her penchant for writing mysteries began upon hearing her mother recite "Humpty Dumpty". At its conclusion, she turned to her mother and said: "Who pushed him?"

If the children focus on the possible voice of the storyteller, the potential meanings in a piece can be explored. One group responded to the challenge of "The Man in the Moon" with these voices: children playing a game, a television newscast complete with anchor desk and on-site-eyewitness reports, and faraway stars gossiping among themselves about the moon man's hasty descent.

An alien from the moon is to meet other aliens on Earth, coordinate location: Norwich. The alien must take human form to survive on this planet. Time is different on the moon and the alien's ship arrived too soon. His alien memory was erased. He looked at his form and believed he was a man and needed sustenance. Before his memory was erased he had time, a little time, to inquire (from a human) directions to Norwich and went south instead of north (direction is reversed on the moon). He chose a popular human food for supper: cold plum porridge. He actually was still an alien and their temperatures are the reverse of earth temperatures. Therefore, he burnt his mouth on cold porridge. If he had come to Earth on time, he would have retained his memory and remembered his purpose. Now he had to remain on Earth until he was discovered missing. Until that time, he had to gradually discover that he had to eat boiling hot human food in order for it to be comfortable for his alien constitution. In time, the aliens abducted him and transformed him to his native appearance and restored his memory.

Jennifer and Joanne, grade four

The children's speculations can lead to an examination of the work of other authors, such as Alison Uttley, whose *Ten Candlelight Tales* are all developed from nursery rhymes, and illustrators such as Maurice Sendak (*Hector Protector*). The remarkable differences in the subjective responses of authors and artists can help encourage the children to trust their judgments, not only of nursery rhymes but of all the poetry they will meet. In addition, children can also recognize how the oral tradition has been and continues to be mined by contemporary writers and artists. We might compare *Each Peach Pear Plum* by Allan and Janet Ahlberg to its traditional sources.

The children can select any two rhymes on a given theme that seem to go together well, and create a new story that incorporates the two existing rhymes and links them together. Afterwards, they can observe how Maurice Sendak attempted this in his remarkable *We're All in the Dumps with Jack and Guy*.

> On Saturday night I lost my wife,
> And where do you think I found her?
> Up in the moon singing a tune,
> With all the stars around her.

Disappearances

Banishment and separatism are severe punishment. But for what? "Owl" in Ted Hughes' book *How the Whale Became and Other Stories* is banished for committing a serious crime. What might explain why the owl in this poem has been banished from a life of comfort and privilege to the wilds of the night and the ivy tree?

> Once I was a monarch's daughter,
>   And sat on a lady's knee;
> But now I am a nightly rover,
>   Banished to the ivy tree.
>
> Crying, Hoo, hoo, hoo, hoo, hoo, hoo,
>   Hoo, hoo, hoo, my feet are cold!
> Pity me, for here you see me
>   Persecuted, poor, and old.

Loss and disappearance can be explored in poems like the following, which are natural springboards for discussion.

> I had two pigeons bright and gay,
> They flew from me the other day;
> What was the reason they did go?
> I cannot tell for I do not know.

I had a little moppet,
I kept it in my pocket
And fed it on corn and hay;
There came a proud beggar
And swore he would wed her,
And stole my little moppet away.
And through the wood she ran, she ran,
And through the wood she ran.
All the long winter she followed the hunter,
And never was heard of again.

Medieval Times

A grade four classroom was working with us, and as the children responded to reading a poem, we were interested in their focus on the language of the rhyme.

I had a little castle upon the seaside;
One half was water, the other was land;
I opened my little castle door, and guess what I found;
I found a fair lady with a cup in her hand.
The cup was gold, and filled with wine;
Drink, fair lady, and thou shalt be mine.

We began by asking about the speaker of the last line, "Drink, fair lady, and thou shalt be mine". One by one, several children stood outside the door, knocked, and when the door was opened, responded in role, revealing different interpretations: a witch who offered a potion; a queen who had been deposed and wanted her power returned; a knight who wanted to marry the lady. (In the task before the role-playing, the class had focused on the term "lady" and decided that it would mean a married woman.) The words "castle", "lady", "thou" and "shalt" caused the children to set the scene in medieval times, determining their choices of role. During the last few minutes of discussion, one child asked if the final line could have been unspoken, just thought by the character handing the cup to the lady, a very sophisticated interpretation, growing from the classroom exploration of the poem.

The children went on to design a medieval-style banner depicting the message of each line of the poem. The banner was divided into four equal parts, telling the poem's story.

Such exploration of the context of rhymes, putting them in a particular time or place, can lead to interesting research and interpretation.

Storytelling

Spontaneous retelling in a circle is one of the most effective ways in which children can reveal what a story rhyme they have just heard has meant to them. With such retelling, no one has the burden of the entire story rhyme. As the story travels around the circle, each participant can add as much or as little as desired. Some children often prefer to pass on the initial round or so until they begin to get more involved in the story. The beauty of this activity is its simplicity and the opportunity it affords each child to put the story rhyme into his or her own words and to make explicit personal story imagery.

> My father died a month ago
> And left me all his riches;
> A feather bed, a wooden leg,
> And a pair of leather breeches;
> A coffee pot without a spout,
> a cup without a handle,
> A tobacco pipe without a lid,
> And half a farthing candle.

In the context of a new rhyme, we often ask the children, in a circle, their feelings and thoughts about the characters. We then may come out of the circle and conduct interviews with each other. "Let's interview this person. Pretend you are a reporter. What would you like to ask? What would you like to know?" That simple technique gets the children talking about the characters. Next, we might have the whole group together, telling stories at once, or we might have a surprise interview with a character, with only three questions, just like the three wishes so common in folktales. Then we help the students to refine their understanding of what they think is important about the story rhyme, arguing and struggling with the three questions that are going to give them the inside information. After that we go back into our storytelling circles and tell the story rhyme one more time, only now we must reveal a big secret that we discovered about the story rhyme that nobody else knows.

Hark, hark, the dogs bark,
The beggars are coming to town;
Some in jags, and some in rags,
And some in velvet gowns.

Some gave them white bread,
And some gave them brown,
And some gave them a good horse-whip,
And sent them out of town.

The beauty of so many nursery rhymes is the strong sense of story they carry. Often, as in this selection, few details are provided, yet much is suggested. To get more from the rhyme, we must take the story and try to do something new with it.

• Try reading this selection in the voices of different storytellers. If nervous town sentries are speaking the lines, the effect will be vastly different than if the voice is that of a raggle-taggle band of wanderers. The children can explore many different possibilities for the voice of the teller.
• Raise questions about the story which, if answered, could offer some interesting insights into the story's possibilities. (For example, is there any reason why these people might be feared?)
• Explore key questions raised by means of interviewing the wanderers. The residents preparing for an influx of wandering beggars can debate whether resisting them or helping them might be the better course of action.
• Write personal memories of the day long ago when the beggar horde converged on the writer's town.

The Opies suggest that this rhyme echoes conditions in Elizabeth's day when wandering beggars were so numerous they were becoming a menace to society:

As G.M. Trevelyan says in his English Social History, 'All through the Tudor reigns, the "beggars are coming to town" preyed on the fears of dwellers in lonely farms and hamlets, and exercised the minds of magistrates, Privy Councillors and Parliaments'. Popular tradition, however, has it that 'the Beggars coming to town' were the Dutchmen in the train of William III, 1688. Beggars is believed to have been, at that time, a common epithet for the Dutch. In this case the 'one in a velvet gown' might refer to William himself.

At the siege of Belle Isle
I was there all the while —
    All the while,
    All the while,
At the siege of Belle Isle.

"At Belle Isle" is another poem which not only evokes a haunting feeling but suggests a good deal more than it actually says. Why are the words "all the while" repeated so often? What effect is created by saying them again and again? Who is the speaker? What has this person gone through?

I went to Noke,
But nobody spoke,
I went to Thame,
It was just the same,
Burford and Brill,
Were silent and still,
But I went to Beckley,
And they spoke directly.

After reading the poem together with the class, it might make an interesting comparison to read Walter de la Mare's poem, "The Listeners". Both pieces evoke feelings of loneliness in the presence of others. Are the towns mentioned in "Noke" all ghost towns, abandoned and left behind, or are the citizens just wary or mistrustful of those they do not know, as appears to be the case in "The Listeners"?

"Is there anybody there?" said the Traveller,
    Knocking on the moonlit door;
And his horse in the silence champed the grasses
    On the forest's ferny floor;
And a bird flew out of the turret,
    Above the Traveller's head:
And he smote upon the door again a second time;
    "Is there anybody there?" he said.
But no one descended to the Traveller;
    No head from the leaf-fringed sill
Leaned over and looked into his grey eyes,
    Where he stood perplexed and still.

But only a host of phantom listeners
    That dwelt in the lone house then
Stood listening in the quiet of the moonlight
    To that voice from the world of men:
Stood thronging the faint moonbeams on the dark stair,
    That goes down to the empty hall,
Hearkening in an air stirred and shaken
    By the lonely Traveller's call.
And he felt in his heart their strangeness,
    Their stillness answering his cry,
While his horse moved, cropping the dark turf,
    'Neath the starred and leafy sky;
For he suddenly smote on the door, even
    Louder, and lifted his head:
"Tell them I came, and no one answered,
    That I kept my word," he said.
Never the least stir made the listeners,
    Though every word he spake
Fell echoing through the shadowiness of the still house
    From the one man left awake:
Ay, they heard his foot upon the stirrup,
    And the sound of iron on stone,
And how the silence surged softly backward,
    When the plunging hoofs were gone.

A class turned the following poem into a movement piece with words as accompaniment. What kind of movements do the words suggest (e.g., slow motion, fast-moving)? A large piece of fabric was used as a backdrop to help create the mood and the presence of the river.

There are men in the village of Erith
Whom nobody seeth or heareth,
    And there looms, on the marge
    Of the river, a barge
That nobody roweth or steereth.

Retelling the Story

One activity that children can find highly stimulating is to retell a story they have read. As they rethink the material, it grows in their imaginations and they come to understand more fully its nooks and crannies, subtleties and surprises. Their ideas about the story of the poem and what it means to them emerge in the retelling. Staying with the story in this way thus facilitates the comprehension process. We should not expect a retold story to remain the same; it will be a resynthesis. Consciously or unconsciously, the teller will make changes to create what seems a better, or more appropriate, story. Listening to others retell the same story helps children examine their own responses with more objectivity. They begin to recognize that their own perceptions are valid, but not absolute. Skilled teachers help young readers build imaginative re-creations of stories in many ways. We must understand both the sensitivity that children bring to a text and the connotations that any story carries for them.

> O, Pearlin Jean!
> O, Pearlin Jean!
> She haunts the hoose,
> She haunts the green,
> An glowers on me
> Wi her wul-cat een.

Is the speaker of these lines frightened? Angry? Frustrated? if you could choose music to accompany the words, what would you select?

Courtney, age fifteen, thought "Pearlin Jean" might be a left-over riddle.

> This is about a candle. A green one. It makes the house glow. Or maybe it's about a canteen a man had in the war. And it haunted him every time he saw it in the house because it saved his life. So he called it Pearlin' Jean. That was the name of his girlfriend.

The story that follows was written by a fourteen-year-old ESL student after reading this poem.

> My Mother said that I never should
> Play with the gypsies in the wood,
> The wood was dark; the grass was green;
> In came Sally with a tambourine.
>
> I went to the sea — no ship to get across;
> I paid ten shillings for a blind white horse;
> I upon his back was off in a crack,
> Sally tell my Mother I shall never come back.

Long time ago, in South America, at a little village, there is a boy named John. he is 15 years old, and he is a really good boy. He helps his mother everything, so his mother think that he is a good guy. She told her neighbour his son is good and how good is his son.

John has a best friend called Sally, they always play together. But one day, there came a gypsy guy, and he changed John's whole life. The gypsy slept in the wood, and John start to play with that gypsy from the second day the gypsy had come. They became friends a few days later, and the gypsy told John about his life, why he wanted to travel around the world, and the things that happened to himself. John felt very interested with all things that gypsy had told him. He had a mind that he want to be like those gypsies, go anywhere they wanted! But John's mother didn't like that gypsy very much, because she thought all the gypsies were the bad people. They don't have their own houses, they sleep everywhere and they are dirty. Still, John kept playing with that gypsy. After that gypsy has gone, the gypsies didn't stay at a same place. They liked to go around the world. John started to feel lonely, even with Sally. He didn't talk to her any more. He started to lose himself.

One day, John went to the sea, but there was no ship for him to get across. Then he found out he had ten shillings, only ten shillings he had. He used it to buy a blind white horse, a blind horse! John knew that, but he lept upon his back and off in a crack! Sally told John's mother, ''I will never come back.'' John wanted to be a gypsy, so he used the only money he had to buy a blind horse, the horse didn't know where he was going. John just wanted to get away, to see how the outside world look like. He didn't want to live in a small village forever. He liked the gypsy life, and he wanted to try how it would be, all the curiosity that made him to left his own place, his mother and also his friend. Nothing was more important than to be a gypsy, to be a really free person.

After 10 years later, John came back to the village, but he didn't stay. Maybe because he said 10 years ago ''I shall never come back.'' But he saw his mother, she had turned old. He still remembered his best friend Sally, but he didn't see her. John's life is not bad. He enjoyed being a gypsy. He saw a lot of things between these 10 years, he studied more things and he knew more things. He didn't repent from being a gypsy. He felt happy about his own choice. John had gone after, he'd gone to continue his gypsy life. He had gone to the other place.

The mysteries of the Booman are ready to be revealed by children who meet the poem:

Ding dong for Booman,
Booman is dead and gone
    Left seven of a family:
    Able and Anthony,
    Richard and Zachary,
James, Thomas, and John.

Where shall we bury him?
    Carry him to London;
By his grandfather's grave
    Grows a green onion.

Dig his grave wide and deep,
    Strew it with flowers;
Toll the bell, toll the bell,
    Twenty-four hours.

Randolph Caldecott

6 * PORTRAITS OF MOTHER GOOSE

Picture book versions of rhymes present invaluable sources for artistic response — the medium used, the style and format, and the point of view of the illustrator can all stimulate non-print activity.

It is often said that television's popularity has resulted in children who are far more adept at responding to visual symbols than to the written word. Whether this is true or not, visual response is an important means of interpreting the world. An appreciation of literature can be developed and motivation increased if we promote the constant harnessing of literature and the visual — in television, film, cartoon, and the children's own work as picture-makers.

Collaborative efforts can draw children together as they plan and work through their ideas and feelings about a story. Sometimes art can be used to further the story response — within a role, as illustration of the writing, as an opportunity to share perceptions. Children can assemble materials that relate to the poems they are exploring, objects mentioned in the lines — collections, maps, facsimiles of journals, letters, advertisements, songs, clothes of the appropriate time. The research that the children collect can add to the context of the story either before or after its being shared, and the information presented can be an experience in itself.

Stepping Out

Sharing a series of portraits from picture books with the children, we can discuss what a portrait is supposed to do: what has the artist done to interest the viewer in the piece? What kind of statements do the portraits make? What feelings do you notice they evoke in you? The children can browse through a selection of Mother Goose "word portraits" and select one to turn into a painting. What clues will they include in the portraits to help the viewer match portrait to rhyme? If we hang all the untitled portraits in an exhibition of Mother Goose we can invite the children to identify or match the portraits to the rhymes.

Gregory Griggs, Gregory Griggs,
Had twenty-seven different wigs.
He wore them up, he wore them down,
To please the people of the town.
He wore them east, he wore them west,
And never could tell which one he liked the best.

Gregory Griggs stepped out with a dazzling variety of hairpieces but didn't seem to get great pleasure from any of them. Can the children design a wig that Gregory just cannot resist? What features of the design will appeal to someone who can't seem to make up his mind? The children can prepare a flyer to send to Gregory that will undoubtedly rouse his curiosity.

Little Jack Horner
Sat in the corner
Eating his Christmas pie,
He put in his thumb,
And pulled out a plum
Saying, What a brave boy am I.

Some "pies" among the nursery rhymes contain strange fillings indeed. What examples can be found? Jack Horner might be a "Tom Thumb" type character. What other adventures might befall one so tiny? Folktales from around the world feature heroes and heroines who are much smaller than those around them. Children can compare their own adventures with tiny characters found in Mother Goose rhymes.

Hector Protector was dressed all in green
Hector Protector was sent to the queen.
The queen did not like him,
No more did the king:
So Hector Protector was sent back again.

The children can brainstorm a list of all the questions this little story does not answer. (Why was he dressed in green? Did he like that colour?) They can then retell the story in the form of a storyboard. (How many scenes will be required not only to deal with the main ideas of the piece, but to supply some answers?) We can share Maurice Sendak's illustrated version *Hector Protector* and *As I Went Over the Water* with the students, comparing the ways they have caught the story with Sendak's version.

> Bobby Shafto's gone to sea,
>   Silver buckles at his knee;
> He'll come back and marry me,
>   Bonny Bobby Shafto!
>
> Bobby Shafto's fat and fair,
>   Combing down his yellow hair;
> He's my love for evermore,
>   Bonny Bobby Shafto!

What elegant fashion parade was rained out and had to be cancelled?

Who stepped out and had a nasty trick played on her?

> Doctor Foster went to Gloucester
> In a shower of rain;
> He stepped in a puddle,
> Right up to his middle,
> And never went there again.

The rhyming of middle with puddle . . . points to the old form of the word piddle having been originally used. Boyd Smith (1920) suggests that the rhyme describes an incident in the travels of Edward I, whose horse, the story goes, once stuck so deep in the mud of a Gloucester street that planks had to be laid on the ground before the creature could regain its footing. Edward is said to have refused ever to visit the city again.

Peter and Iona Opie

A group of eight-year-olds told this version:

- Dr. Foster was walking to a grocery store in Gloucester to get a special homeopathic soup for his sick wife (because he was a homeopathic doctor).

- He walked because his car was broken.
- Because he had to walk, he took a short cut through a quarry (when he drives his car he takes a different route).
- He decided to go out after a heavy rain storm.
- There were no warning signs around the quarry so he stepped in the narrow, deep puddle thinking that it was just a small shallow puddle but he ended up in water up to his waist ("middle").
- In the end, he decided that he would never go that route to the grocery store again, but stick with his normal route in the car.

Famous Players

> Hannah Bantry
> in the pantry
> Gnawing on a mutton bone,
> How she gnawed it,
> How she clawed it,
> When she found herself alone.

A group of children looked through magazines for pictures they thought could be cut out to suggest or interpret the poem "Hannah Bantry." When the composite portraits were complete, the children mounted their creations with masking tape across the chalkboard. Then they examined all the pieces of art and began to notice similarities and differences.

As a class, the children began to classify and categorize the faces: those that seemed frightened, those that appeared lonely, those that loved food, those that were happy, and so on. The children were examining responses to the story poem, building a world of personal interpretation and adding to their own singular visions by sharing perceptions, helping each other examine critically, and coming to understand the general principles of building bigger story worlds through interaction.

> Call John the boatman,
> Call, call again,
> For loud flows the river
> And fast falls the rain.
> John is a good man, and sleeps very sound;

His oars are at rest, and his boat is aground.
Fast flows the river so rapid and deep;
The louder you call him, the sounder he'll sleep.

One class of nine-year-olds co-constructed the story of John the boatman using all the clues in the old rhyme. They decided the story was about a person named John, a boatman, who sleeps very soundly and:

- lives by a lake;
- fixes boats;
- is a fisherman.
- The sound of waves doesn't make John worry and he can sleep.
- He is used to the river being very loud and splashing against the rocks so he can sleep soundly even in the face of loud noises.
- It sounds like a river you go rafting on.
- It is night time and John is sleeping and it is raining outside.
- Someone is calling him to fix boats.
- The river may be calling him.
- He's on vacation, resting, from the water.
- Sleep doesn't necessarily mean he's sleeping. It could mean he's just not out on the water.

A Collection of Characters

In Michael Foreman's illustrated Mother Goose, characters appear and then reappear several pages later. The rhymes are displayed as in a narrative and children delight in recognizing and connecting the events and the people as the book is shared. With the following collection of poems, children can create Mother Goose's village, beginning with a large map of the locale, and placing each character's name somewhere in the village. Groups of children can take ownership of each rhyme, creating a "life space" for each character, depicting their situations, homes, relationships, problems, and joys, and showing the connections from one to another, so that a village begins to take shape in the classroom, and stories can be told about the various villagers and their fables and fortunes. The information could be enclosed in a scrapbook or displayed graphically on a map. Nursery rhyme characters are often "wise fools" silly in their simple ways, but sometimes archetypal in their complexities.

Each village will appear unique in its classroom setting, and each group of children will reflect and reveal their own experiences inside its limits. The world of Mother Goose can become a collection of characters as painted and pictured by today's children.

Dingty diddlety,
    My mammy's maid,
She stole oranges,
    I am afraid;
Some in her pocket,
    Some in her sleeve,
She stole oranges,
    I do believe.

William McTrimbletoe,
He's a good fisherman,
Catches fishes,
Puts them in dishes,
Catches hens,
Puts them in pens;
Some lay eggs,
Some lay none,
William McTrimbletoe
He doesn't eat one.

Pretty John Watts,
    We are troubled with rats,
Will you drive them out of the house?
    We have mice, too, in plenty,
    That feast in the pantry;
    But let them stay,
    And nibble away:
What harm is a little brown mouse?

Cobbler, cobbler, mend my shoe,
Yes, good master, that I'll do.
Stitch it up and stitch it down,
And then I'll give you half a crown.

Cobbler, cobbler, mend my shoe,
Get it done by half-past two;
Half-past two, it can't be done,
Get it done by half-past one.

Follow my Bangalorey Man,
Follow my Bangalorey Man,
I'll do all that ever I can,
To follow my Bangalorey Man,
We'll borrow a horse, and steal a gig,
And round the world we'll do a jig,
And I'll do all that ever I can,
To follow my Bangalorey Man.

Oh! cruel was the press-gang
    That took my love from me;
Oh! cruel was the little ship
    That took him out to sea;
And cruel was the splinter-board
    That took away his leg;
Now he is forced to fiddle-scrape,
    And I am forced to beg.

The following three poems are all connected by theme and
phrase.

Desperate Dan
The dirty old man
Washed his face
In a frying-pan;
Combed his hair
With the leg of a chair;
Desperate Dan
The dirty old man.

Who are you?
A dirty old man.
I've always been
since the day I began,
Mother and Father
were dirty before me,
Hot or cold water
has never come o'er me.

My son John is a nice old man,
Washed his face in a frying-pan,
Combed his hair with a wagon-wheel,
And died with the toothache in his heel.

Nursery Rhyme Folk: Developing a Thematic Unit

Nursery rhymes represent centuries of literature, skipping along with rhythm and rhyme and bits of historical wit. Mixed in Mother Goose's treasure bag are countless women who have peopled the playgrounds of this oral heritage. By focusing on these outrageous, terrible, comic, and sad rhyming characters, we can couple the traditional English verse with images that reflect the spirit, the fun, the pain of contemporary living. These nursery rhyme women live again in word and picture for today's children. Together, we can observe these rhymes, and find these women's stories buried in the remnants of words centuries old. The children can discover and create lives for these women, illuminating the stereotypes so often conjured up in old verses, and replacing them with more complex characters.

> Nursery rhymes still feature some lively females, who do their own work, disobey some of the rules, and are not always as easily married off as their critics have sometimes implied. They offer a lively and occasionally outspoken commentary on the male-female relationship in many of its aspects, often more vividly than is the case in other kinds of children's literature.
>
> Nicholas Tucker

Different groups that have explored various aspects of a theme or topic in the rhymes may want to hear from each other to expand their knowledge. They can transfer their findings to scripts, overhead transparencies, or large charts and share the information.

There was an old woman who had three sons,
   Jerry and James and John.
Jerry was hung and James was drowned,
John was lost and never was found,
So there was an end of her three sons,
   Jerry and James and John.

This is the first of fourteen verses in *The Old Woman and Her Three Sons*, a toy book with coloured illustrations published by John Harris in 1815. It is a verse that was certainly current in the reign of Charles I, and may go back to Elizabeth I's time.

A grade seven class made several astute observations about this poem:

- The woman is never named. Was she insignificant or was the focus on the three men?
- At first, they thought the men were criminals, but then the discussion turned toward their having been rebels or outsiders, destroyed by civil unrest.
- Was John lost psychologically, or did he leave the family for some reason?
- Could the old woman represent England, and the names of the three men countries or colonies?
- Was the absence of grief by the woman due to the times in which she lived — constant loss and death of children due to the plague, wars and poverty?

The children hitchhiked on each other's ideas, and gradually settled on the metaphor of the country being represented by the "old woman", a complex bit of poetic analysis.

Another version:

There was an old woman had three cows,
    Rosy and Colin and Dun.
Rosy and Colin were sold at the fair,

And Dun broke her heart in a fit of despair,
So there was an end of her three cows,
    Rosy and Colin and Dun.

A group of grade seven children interpreted the following poem in a variety of ways:

There was an old woman,
had nothing,
And there came thieves,
to rob her,
And when she cried,
she made no sound,
But all the country heard her.

- *I got the idea that the lady was very poor and looked upon as useless. I think of the thieves as "spirits of death" and they rob her of her life. She cries silently as she makes her final prayer and then she dies peacefully. The country hears through gossip and they pity her death. I get a feeling of sorrow, yet a lot of sympathy.*

Janice

- *rich lady who had nothing emotionally*
- *nothing to show for her life*
- *nothing/nobody in her life*
- *country understood her and felt her pain*
- *she made no sound because she had no one to listen to her*

Anne, Helen, Kiara, Desta

- *the poem is about vengence against the woman*
- *the old woman is mother nature, and the thieves are humans destroying the earth*

Andrew, Michael, Wesley

- *old woman was a martyr*
- *The thieves came to rob — she had nothing — so took her life. Being a martyr, she died silently — but news of her horrific death, was all around the country*
- *When the thieves came and robbed her, she made no sound but it was in the news and she resurfaced*

Leah

- *I think thieves came, and she told them she had nothing*
- *they saw something that probably wasn't really valuable, but had high sentimental value to her*
- *they tried to steal it but she stopped them*
- *they told her they would kill her, but she said nothing*
- *they killed her while she cried to God, and the whole country heard her*

Jennifer

It means that she was attempted to be robbed by highway men, although she had nothing. But it was witnessed by a noble, and although she made but a weak sound, the news spread throughout the land.

Jeremy, Mike, Al

There are several other nursery rhymes which seem to have stemmed from this verse, such as this one:

There was a man and he had nought,
    And robbers came to rob him;
He crept up to the chimney top,

And then they thought they had him.
But he got down on the other side,
    And then they could not find him;
He ran fourteen miles in fifteen days,
    And never looked behind him.

An Anthology of Women

Here's a poor widow from Babylon,
With six poor children all alone;
One can bake, and one can brew,
One can shape, and one can sew,
One can sit at the fire and spin,
One can bake a cake for the king;
    Come choose you east,
    Come choose you west,
    Come choose the one
    You love the best.

There was an old woman of Surrey,
Who was morn, noon, and night in a hurry;
Called her husband a fool,
Drove her children to school,
The worrying old woman of Surrey.

There was an old woman of Norwich,
Who lived upon nothing but porridge;
    Parading into town,
    She turned cloak into gown,
The thrifty old woman of Norwich.

The old woman must stand
    At the tub, tub, tub,
The dirty clothes
    To rub, rub, rub;
But when they are clean
    And fit to be seen,
She'll dress like a lady,
    And dance on the green.

There was an old woman, and what do you think?
She lived upon nothing but victuals and drink:
Victuals and drink were the chief of her diet,
And yet this old woman could never keep quiet.

She went to the baker, to buy her some bread,
And when she came home, her old husband was dead;
She went to the clerk to toll the bell,
And when she came back her old husband was well.

A famous old woman was Madam McBight,
She slept all day, she slept all night,
One hour was given to victuals and drink,
And only a minute was taken to think.

There was an old woman
Liv'd under a hill,
And if she isn't gone,
She lives there still.

Baked apples she sold,
And cranberry pies,
And she's the old woman
That never told lies.

There was an old woman
    who lived in Dundee,
And in her back garden
    There grew a plum tree;
The plums they grew rotten
    Before they grew ripe,
And she sold them
    Three farthings a pint.

There was an old woman
    and nothing she had,
And so this old woman
    Was said to be mad.
She'd nothing to eat,
    She'd nothing to wear,
She'd nothing to lose,
    She'd nothing to fear,
She'd nothing to ask,
    And nothing to give,
And when she did die
    She'd nothing to leave.

How can we explore with children the snapshots of the lives
of the women captured in these nursery rhymes. As Nicholas
Tucker has suggested, many of these female characters have

survived under terrible circumstances, and the children can begin to fill in the missing pieces of the puzzles, through discussion, role play, painting or storytelling.

- How did each woman in a rhyme arrive at her present situation?
- What went wrong/or right along the way?
- What obstacles did she overcome?
- Did any difficulties overwhelm her?
- What stories could she now tell? Does she?
- What other tales do people tell about her?
- Where does she live now? Does she have any possessions?
- Does she dream of changing her life, or has she accepted her loss?
- At a community function — a wedding or a funeral — does she participate?
- Does she have any special friends?
- Do strangers seek her out?

The children could share their stories of these Nursery Rhyme Women and look for similarities and differences in the creations. Perhaps the women could be interviewed about their lives through role play, one group questioning a member of another group as the lady in question.

Versioning

> There was a mad man,
> And he had a mad wife,
> And they lived all in a mad lane!
> They had three children all at a birth,
> And they too were mad every one.
> The father was mad,
> The mother was mad,
> The children all mad beside;
> And upon a mad horse they all of them got,
> And madly away did ride.

A grade eight class examined the complexity of the term "mad" in this poem, recognizing its importance through its repetitive use. Some felt the family was insane, genes passed on by the parents to the children (all of this turmoil causing the horse to behave erratically). Others decided the family was eccentric, hounded by villagers because of their differences — their physical features, religious attitudes, philosophy of life, and so on. One youngster revealed that he thought they were riding to Hell, crazed by the predicaments of their lives. In fact, another verse offered by one researcher says that they went to Hell, and were so difficult that the devil expelled them.

Members of the class continued to hold these various positions concerning the description of the families, and each left the classroom attempting to dissuade the other.

Another group wanted to know if the women in her family — mother, grandmother, sisters, etc. — were under a spell. What terrible events had occurred in their lives? How could the misery be stopped? Could the spell be passed on through generations?

Long ago, multiple births were viewed with some suspicion. It was thought, for example, that a mother of twins had been guilty of having intercourse with two men, and a mother of triplets with three. The class discussed the implications of this for the poem.

In his book *Culture Shock* Michael Rosen includes this epitaph from a woman who could no longer cope.

In 1905, Catherine Alsopp, a Sheffield washerwoman, composed her own epitaph before hanging herself:

Here lies a poor woman who always was tired;
She lived in a house where help was not hired,
Her last words on earth were: 'Dear friends, I am going
Where washing ain't done, nor sweeping, nor sewing.
But everything there is exact to my wishes,
For where they don't eat, there's no washing of dishes.
I'll be where loud anthems will always be ringing
But having no voice, I'll be clear of the singing.
Don't mourn for me now, don't mourn for me never,
I'm going to do nothing for ever and ever.

The children can progress with "versioning", developing their own story from a story they have heard or read. They can settle place, time, characters, details, mood, style, technique.

A visual timeline can be built by the readers to represent these poems. For example, incidents from a poem can be drawn and hung on a clothesline in the sequence in which they occurred in the invented narrative.

The children can also magnify one small detail or incident in their story and prepare a close-up view of their vision of it. It may be a vignette only briefly mentioned, or a place not described, or an incident just referred to.

Pictures can accompany the stories created by the children as they stand on the shoulders of the stories they have heard or read. One child may illustrate another's work, causing the two to share details of interpretation, so that the story and illustrations are a collaborative effort.

Arthur Rackham

7 * ORGANIZING MOTHER GOOSE

Creating an Anthology

It may be beneficial to encourage children, especially older ones for whom the nursery rhymes are not familiar ground, to create their own Mother Goose anthologies based on patterns of organization which appeal to them. Whether the rhymes are gathered by subject (cats, work, eating), types of rhyme (tongue twisters, riddles, game rhymes), themes (big and little, wise and foolish), or patterns of discourse (conversations, declarations, exclamations) or any other possibilities the children find for juxtaposing the selections, some quite exciting discoveries can be made. Children can classify poems by the opinions represented. They can arrange poems by viewpoint, attitude, behaviour, religion, ethics, morality. They can translate the form of the poem into other types of writing — monologues, scripts, or vice versa. They need to find rhymes that link together in some way. They could examine *Michael Foreman's Mother Goose* to find out how the double-page spreads offer many ideas for layout and design.

After reading the poems, the teacher can ask the children for the words they liked, the way the words made them feel, and how the words sounded special. These can be put on a chart and categorized and classified. The children can list their favourite words and phrases, the rhymes they enjoy, the pictures that are the best, the metaphors and the comparisons they will remember.

Children may want to write up their own questions about the poems that can become the focus of groupwork or class discussion. They may jot down their thoughts and feelings as they are reading each poem, almost in a stream of consciousness with associations, connotations, and reflections. This may help the children to understand their own processes of reading poetry and contribute to the discussion after the poems have been read.

A poem can be shared without a title; the children can then decide on an appropriate or possible title after re-reading the poem. Titles can be suggested, discussed, and voted upon.

Once collections have been assembled, the children can concentrate on what images, thoughts, and feelings pass through their minds or what memories are triggered by the assemblage. Images and words torn from magazines can then be put into collages which would illustrate the anthologies. Some students may prefer to explore sound collages, arranging their anthologies for oral performance by solo and chorus voices. Examples of musical collages (e.g., Ravel's Mother Goose Suite) might also be introduced.

The children can plan and execute a mural of a Mother Goose village by incorporating six rhymes into the design.

> Robin the Bobbin,
>   the big-bellied Ben,
> He ate more meat
>   than fourscore men;
> He ate a cow,
>   he ate a calf,
> He ate an ox
>   and a half,
> He ate a church,
>   he ate a steeple,
> He ate a priest
>   and all the people!
> A cow and a calf,
> An ox and a half,
> A church and a steeple,
> And all the good people,
> And yet he complained
>   that his stomach wasn't full.

This poem echoes a similar theme:

> There was an old woman called Nothing-at-all,
> Who lived in a dwelling exceedingly small;
> A man stretched his mouth to its utmost extent,
> And down at one gulp house and old woman went.

112

Alison Lurie says that in life, as in folklore, children reveal through dreams that they are afraid of two things — being abandoned and being devoured.

Folktales featuring a wicked creature who repeatedly swallows victims until fit to burst are not difficult to find. (e.g., *The Terrible Tiger* by Jack Prelutsky; *The Fat Cat* by Jack Kent; *The Clay Pot Boy* by Cynthia Jameson). How is the orgy of gobbling usually halted in such stories? ''Robin the Bobbin'' resembles the classic swallowing tale in many respects. However, we don't know what sent him on the rampage and the ending still has him on the loose. The discussion and drawings that grow from the rhymes offer opportunities for exploring these issues in the light of day.

Romance

Little maid, pretty maid, whither goest thou?
    Down in the forest to milk my cow.
Shall I go with thee? No, not now.
    When I send for thee then come thou.

In some parts of England to ask a girl if one might go milking with her was considered tantamount to a proposal of marriage.

''Auld wife, auld wife,
Will ye go-a-shearin?''
''Speak a wee bit looder, sir,
I'm unco dull o'hearin.''

''Auld wife, auld wife,
Wad ye tak a kiss?''
''Aye, indeed, I wull, sir;
I wadna be amiss.''

One I love,
Two I love,
Three I love, I say,
Four I love with all my heart,
Five I cast away;
Six he loves me,
Seven he don't,
Eight we're lovers both;
Nine he comes,

Ten he tarries,
Eleven he courts.
Twelve he marries.

Bad news is come to Town, bad news is carry'd,
Bad news is come to Town, my Love is Mary'd.

He loves me,
He don't!
He'll have me.
He won't!
He would if he could.
But he can't
So he don't.

This last bit of sad sorrowful verse is called a lament. Skim
through a collection of nursery rhymes to find other examples
of laments. Do modern poets write laments? The children could
search through some collections of poetry by individual authors
and try to find an example of a poem that might be described
as a lament.

Here are some titles to help you get started:

My Underwear's Inside Out by Diane Dawber;
Come On into My Tropical Garden by Grace Nichols;
Auntie's Knitting A Baby by Lois Simmie
I Want to Lasso Time by George Swede;
The Word Party by Richard Edwards;
All Day Saturday by Charles Causley;
Beams by Vyanne Samuels.

Canary Friends

Little Clotilda, well and hearty,
Thought she'd like to give a party.
But her friends were shy and wary.
Nobody came but her own canary.

This ten-year-old's response demonstrates an awareness of the
stories behind the poem:

The first thing that comes to my mind is how friends play a big
role in our life. In times of need, in times of joy, in time of

sorrow, you usually go to a friend. And when you want to have a party, you invite your friends. Unfortunately, though, in this case, I don't think that Clotilda has met her real friends yet. She needs friends who are fun and outgoing like herself. This was probably written by Clotilda herself because it gives me the feeling of sadness, loneliness, and even some pity for Clotilda.

Rick

The poet Rita Ann Higgins approaches Clotilda's canary from a different perspective.

WHAT IS A CANARY?

Hippolyta O'Hara
would like to own
a mare called Bella.

But where would she keep her,
she lives in a housing estate,
no mares named Bella allowed.

Hippolyta O'Hara
would like to own
a minotaur called Harry.

But where would she keep him,
she lives in a housing estate,
no minotaurs named Harry allowed.

Hippolyta O'Hara
would like to own
a crocodile called Leonard.

But where would she keep him,
she lives in a housing estate,
no crocodiles named Leonard allowed.

Hippolyta O'Hara
would like to own
a canary called Dominico,
but the cat would eat him.

"What about the housing estate?"

A canary is a canary
in a housing estate
or in a bishop's house.

The cat is the problem.

And what will the children think about Mary and her canary?

Mary had a pretty bird,
    Feathers bright and yellow,
slender legs, upon my word,
    He was a pretty fellow.

The sweetnest notes he always sung,
    Which much delighted Mary;
And near the cage she'd ever sit,
    To hear her own canary.

A menagerie of creatures could be the stimulus for a collection of rhymes drawn from several classroom anthologies, and depicted on a display board or in a large class book: snails, cows, robins, frogs, foxes, flies, dogs, cats, donkeys, roosters — all live in Mother Goose's world.

Seasons

The north wind doth blow,
And we shall have snow,
And what will poor Robin do then?
    Poor thing.
He'll sit in a barn,
And keep himself warm,
And hide his head under his wing,
    Poor thing.

This poem is famous for the powerful sense of winter and cold it evokes. Using it as a beginning, the children can find poems that capture strong feelings of this season. Christina Rossetti, William Shakespeare, and Charles Causley are a few poets who have written of winter's cold.

AFTERWORD

For hundreds of years, nursery rhymes have provided children with unique language patterns and word play, unfamiliar yet intriguing, and we are grateful for them. The intricacies of these rhymes let us work our tongues, lips, and vocal chords towards the goals of delight and surprise. The treasure trove of the English language is contained in sayings from Mother Goose, the rhymes join us with the past, integrate us with the present, and lift us into the future. We as adults can revisit childhood accompanied by youngsters who are living through the moment with the rhymes of another century. Of course, we ourselves enjoy the discovery of new rhymes and the rediscovery of old familiar ones. And each of us meets each poem with different eyes and sensitivities.

Just as the writing of Milton and Shakespeare lets us own joyous words and ideas from the past, Mother Goose fills our memories with leftover bits and pieces that echo the voices of nannies and nurses and teachers and parents and poets and playwrights, all filtered through the years and years of children who blinked and laughed and cried at grown-ups, connecting us in a moment with every language learner who ever fell under the spell of Mother Goose.

Perhaps, after all of your work with nursery rhymes, you will be able to take a collection from the shelf, open it up, read the verses aloud and charm the children as Terence McDiddler charmed the fish from the sea.

Terence McDiddler,
   The three-stringed fiddler,
Can charm, if you please,
   The fish from the seas.

SELECTED READING

Agard, John, and Nichols, Grace. *No Hickory. No Dickory. No Dock.* Harmondsworth: Puffin 1991.
  • A lively collection of Caribbean nursery rhymes for younger children.

Alderson, Brian, and Oxenbury, Helen. *Cakes and Custard.* London: Heinemann, 1974.
  • Some interesting variations on familiar nursery rhymes accompanied by Helen Oxenbury's wonderful comic portraits. A wonderful collection.

Baring-Gould, William and Ceil. *The Annotated Mother Goose.* New York: Bramhall House, 1962.
  • This gathering containing more than one thousand rhymes, from the earliest surviving publications to the present day, is the most complete collection ever assembled. The rhymes are usually given in their earliest published form, which was often later suppressed (what was common in the 18th century was later thought too bawdy) and the authors have included most of the known variations the originals.

Bayley, Nicola. *Nicola Bayley's Book of Nursery Rhymes.* Harmondsworth: Puffin, 1984.
  • Beautifully detailed visuals make this a handsome book to linger over.

Blake, Quentin. *Quentin Blake's Nursery Rhyme Book.* Harmondsworth: Puffin, 1986.
  • Sixteen lesser known rhymes are vigorously expanded in Blake's witty and ebullient style.

Briggs, Raymond. *The Mother Goose Treasury.* London: Hamish Hamilton, 1987.
  • An earthly, boisterous all round satisfying collection of

nursery verse. Not a dull moment in this wonderful collection of over 400 rhymes and 1000 illustrations

Causley, Charles. *All Day Saturday*. New York: Macmillan, 1994.
- A collection of poems from one of England's most distinguished poets. Classically illustrated by Anthony Lewis.

Causley, Charles. *Early in the Morning*. New York: Viking, 1986.
- Forty poems and rhymes perfectly blend the sound of traditional verse with Causley's own intense originality.

Cooney, Barbara. *Tortillitas para Mama and Other Nursery Rhymes in Spanish and English*. New York: Holt, Rinehart and Winston, 1981.
- These Latin American rhymes have been passed on orally from generation to generation. They have been lovingly gathered and translated for this book.

de la Mare, Walter. *Peacock Pie: A Book of Rhymes*. London: Faber and Faber, 1993.
- This edition contains perhaps the very finest of Walter de la Mare's poems for children.

de Paola, Tomie. *Mother Goose*. New York: Putnam, 1985.
- More than two hundred rhymes drawn with Tomie de Paola's gentle, even style.

Farjeon, Eleanor. *Invitation to a Mouse and other poems*. London: Hodder & Stoughton, 1983.
- A collection of the poems of Eleanor Farjeon that echo her love of nursery rhymes.

Foreman, Michael. *Michael Foreman's Mother Goose*. London: Macmillan, 1988.
- Mother Goose rhymes are organized thematically on colourful double-page spreads. Great fun!

Harrowven, Jean. *The Origins of Rhymes, Songs and Sayings*. London: Kaye & Ward, 1977.
- Jean Harrowven gives an eminently readable account of rhymes' origins and development from pre-Christian times to the present day, as well as much background information about each period.

Himler, Ron. *The Bedtime Mother Goose*. New York: Golden Press, 1980.
- Twenty-five nursery rhymes based on the theme of getting ready for bed and the world of dreams.

Kroll, Virginia. *An African Mother Goose*. Illustrated by Katherine Roundtree. Maine: Charlesbridge Publishing, 1995.

- These rhymes portray the cultures of Africa while preserving the rhythm and rhyme of traditional Mother Goose favourites.

Lee, Dennis. *The Ice Cream Store*. Toronto: HarperCollins, 1991.

Lee, Dennis. *Jelly Belly*. Toronto: Macmillian, 1983.

- A collection of modern poems that are just as playful and hilarious as the original nursery rhymes we all remember.

Lines, Kathleen. *Lavender's Blue*. Oxford.

- Perhaps not as exciting as some of the more recent nursery rhyme collections, yet a sterling collection with wonderful watercolours by Harold Jones.

Lobel, Arnold. *Arnold Lobel's Book of Mother Goose*. New York: Random House, 1986.

- Illustrating three hundred selections from Mother Goose, Lobel calls the verses a "lively, lusty body of literature" that has all too often been given interpretations that are "so polite, so genteel, so well-behaved. My concept of Mother Goose is just the opposite: bawdy and naughty."

Lobel, Arnold. *Gregory Griggs and Other Nursery Rhyme People*. Greenwillow Books, New York, 1978.

- The creator of Frog, Toad, Owl, Mr. Muster and other immortal characters introduces us to a circle of new friends, painting them with the humor, tenderness and dicernment that have made him one of the leading picture book artists of our time.

Lottridge, Celia. *Mother Goose: A Canadian Sampler*. Toronto: Douglas & McIntyre, 1994.

- This collection was published for the benefit of the Parent-Child Mother Goose Program. Established in 1986 to introduce mothers and fathers who need support in parenting to the joys of play and language as exemplified by the canon of work known as Mother Goose, the program is an exciting and innovative approach to developing parenting skills. Twenty-nine of Canada's best-loved children's illustrators agreed to donate artwork to the collection, each choosing a rhyme to illustrate.

Lurie, Alison. *Don't tell the grownups: Subversive children's literature*. Boston: Little Brown, 1990.

- The author examines some of the controversies in contemporary children's books.

Matterson, Elizabeth. *This Little Puffin* (revised edition). Harmondsworth: Puffin, 1991.
- A comprehensive collection of finger plays, action rhymes, play rhymes, nursery rhymes and just about every other rhyme imaginable.

Meek, Margaret. *On Being Literate*. London: The Bodley Head, 1991.
- An engaging personal view by a respected authority of literacy and literature and children.

Merriam, Eve. *The Inner City Mother Goose*. New York: Simon and Schuster, 1975.
- A gathering of nursery rhymes altered from their classic form to dramatize the desperation of life in urban ghettos.

Montgomerie, Norah and William. *Scottish Nursery Rhymes*. Chambers, 1985.
- Norah and William Montgomerie have gathered over two hundred traditional rhymes from all over Scotland. There are games, counting rhymes, songs, lullabies, riddles, even toasts.

Opie, Iona and Peter. *The Puffin Book of Nursery Rhymes*. Harmondsworth: Puffin, 1963.
- A handy reference for the teacher's desk.

Opie, Iona and Peter. *The Oxford Nursery Rhyme Book*. London: Oxford, 1955.
- One of the most comprehensive of the nursery rhyme collections — and the best.

Opie, Iona and Peter. *The Oxford Dictionary of Nursery Rhymes*. London: Oxford, 1951.
- This volume chronicles the extensive work that lies behind the Opie collections. Detailed notes and information accompany the rhymes.

Opie, Iona. *Tail Feathers from Mother Goose*. London: Walker Books, 1994.
- These rhymes have been chosen by Iona Opie from the Opie family archives, built up over forty years. Almost all are previously unpublished: they are unusual versions of known nursery rhymes or versions sent by correspondents or used by the Opies themselves, which became transformed, in Iona

Opie's words, "because Opies cannot remember anything straight."

Ormerod, Jan. *Rhymes around the Day*. Harmondsworth: Puffin, 1983.
- a day in the life of a modern family is highlighted by traditional nursery rhymes.

Potter, Beatrix. *Beatrix Potter's Nursery Rhyme Book*. London: Frederick Warne, 1984.
- Beatrix Potter was inordinately fond of nursery rhymes and riddles, weaving them into her tales whenever she could. This is a collection of her favourite rhymes.

Prelutsky, Jack. *A Nonny Mouse Writes Again!* New York: Knopf, 1993.
- Here are more than fifty of M. Mouse's funniest, shortest, and easiest to memorize poems, selected by Mr. Prelutsky for their perfect read-aloud quality.

Prelutsky, Jack. *Ride a Purple Pelican*. New York: Greenwillow, 1986.
- Jack Prelutsky and Garth Williams have created a nursery rhyme world peopled with unforgettable characters.

Provensen, Alice and Martin. *The Mother Goose Book*. New York: Random House, 1976.
- A handsomely illustrated themed collection of more than 160 rhymes.

Scieszka, Jon. *The Book That Jack Wrote*. New York: Viking, 1994.
- "It's about a Rat, a Cat, a cow over the moon, and a Baby humming a tune. it's about what the Bug did to the rug. It's about how the Egg fell off the wall. It's about nursery rhymes and chaos."

Sendak, Maurice. *We Are All in the Dumps with Jack and Guy*. New York: HarperCollins, 1993.
- Sendak combines two nursery rhymes to create an epic tale of the plight of poor children in the closing years of the twentieth century.

Sharon, Lois and Bram. *Sharon, Lois & Bram's Mother Goose*. Toronto: Douglas & McIntyre, 1985.
- A collection of songs, nursery rhymes, tickling verses and games for children from six months to seven years. A song book, a picture book, and a read-aloud rhyme book.

Steward Fraser, Amy. *Dae ye Min' Langsyne? A Pot pourri of Games, Rhymes and Plays of Scottish Childhood.* London: Routledge & Kegan Paul, 1975.

- A collection of personal memories of childhood from over one hundred contributors. Their memories of the games they played, and the words they sang and said, provide a fascinating and unusual view of the child's world.

Stones, Rosemary, and Mann, Andrew. *Mother Goose Comes to Cable Street.* Harmondsworth: Penguin, 1979.

- The old nursery rhymes are presented here in a twentieth-century inner city context — multicultural London.

Tripp, Wallace. *Marguerite, Go Wash Your Feet.* Boston: Little, Brown, 1985.

- These nonsense rhymes from Mother Goose are a treat for any child.

Tripp, Wallace. *Granfa' Grig Had a Pig.* Boston: Little, Brown, 1976.

- Comical rendering of over one hundred favourite rhymes with cameo appearances by such famous folks as Princess Anne, Robert Frost, Napoleon Bonaparte, Harold Lloyd and others.

Voake, Charlotte. *Over the Moon.* London: Walker, 1985.

- A wide assortment of rhymes accompanied by Charlotte Voake's humorous illustrations.

Watson, Wendy. *Wendy Watson's Mother Goose.* New York: Lothrop, Lee & Sheppard, 1989.

- The cycles of a day and a year create a pattern for organizing Mother Goose rhymes.

Wildsmith, Brian. *Mother Goose.* Oxford University Press, 1963.

- Bold, brightly illustrated rhymes as only Wildsmith can render them.

Wyndham, Robert. *Chinese Mother Goose Rhymes.* New York: Putnam, 1968.

- A collection of nursery rhymes translated from Chinese, including ones on lady bugs, kites, and bumps on the head. Also includes the rhymes in Chinese characters.

Yolen, Jane. *Jane Yolen's Mother Goose Songbook.* Honesdale, Pennsylvania: Boyd's Mills Press, 1992.

- More than forty-five nursery rhymes and accompanying musical arrangements are included in this collection. In addition, all the rhymes have been annotated.

Yolen, Jane. *Street Rhymes around the World*. Honesdale, Pennsylvania: Boyd's Mills Press, Inc., 1992.
- An illustrated anthology of jump-rope and other counting street rhymes from seventeen countries.

PUBLISHING
ACKNOWLEDGEMENTS

Every effort has been made to contact copyright holders. In the event of an inadvertent ommission or error, please contact the publisher at Pembroke Publishers Limited, 538 Hood Road, Markham, Ontario, Canada, L3R 3K9.

For permission to reprint the poems and excerpts included in this book, acknowledgement is made as follows:

"The Owl," "John Boatman," "The Chatelaine," from *Tail Feathers from Mother Goose*, Walker Books Ltd., London.

Agard, John, "Pumpkin, Pumpkin," from *No Hickory, No Dickory, No Dock*, Puffin Books, London.

Aylesworth, John, "Yellow Yellow Sunup," from *My Son John*, Henry Holt & Company, New York.

Benson, Gerard, "Once When I Wasn't Very Big," from *The Magnificent Callisto*, Blackie Children's Books, Penguin, London.

Causley, Charles, "One for the Man," from *Early in the Morning*, Viking-Kestrel/Viking Children's Books, London.

Curry, Jennifer, ed., "Sea Swan," "Baby Breakfast," "Old Man Wind," "What's that down there?" "My Brother Barry," from *The Best of Children's Poetry*, a Red Fox Book, Random House, London.

Demi, "The Mighty Emperor Ch'in Shih Huang," from *Dragon Kites and Dragonflies: A Collection of Chinese Nursery Rhymes*, Harcourt Brace and Company, New York.

Griego, Margot, et al., "Sleep My Child," from *Tortillitas Para Moma & Other Spanish Rhymes*, Harcourt Brace & Company, New York.

Hoban, Russell, "Old Man Ocean," from *The Pedalling Man*, Heinemann Young Books, London.

Janeczko, Paul, "Ten Little Aliens," from *Poetry from A to Z*. Simon & Schuster Publishers, New York.

Jones, Dan, illustrator, "When I Was a Little Boy" from Rosemary Stones and Andrew Mann, *Mother Goose Comes to Cable Street*, Kestrel Books, Penguin, London.

Kushkin, Karla, "Thirty Thirsty Thistles," from *The Rose in My Coke*, Harper Collins Publishers, Toronto.

Lee, Dennis, "I'm Sailing to Sea in the Bathroom," from *Jelly Belly*, MacMillan Publishers, Toronto.

Lee, Dennis, "The Question," from *Nicholas Knock and Other People — Poems*, Sterling Lord Associates, Toronto.

Lee, Dennis, "Lucy Go Lightly," from *The Ice Cream Store*, Harper Collins Publishers, Toronto.

Merriam, Eve, "One Misty Moisty Morning," from *The Inner City Mother Goose*, New York: Simon & Schuster.

Rosen, Michael, "One," from *Mind the Gap*, Scholastic, London.

Watson, Wendy, "How Many Miles to Newburyport?" from *Catch Me and Kiss Me and Say It Again*, Harper Collins Publishers, New York.